The Real Faith

Original Pentecostal Classics Edition

By
Dr. Charles S. Price

With Forward and Introduction By
Tim Enloe

E M Publications
Wichita, KS

THE REAL FAITH:
Original Pentecostal Classics Edition

By Charles S. Price with Forward and
Introduction By Tim Enloe

© 2008 Enloe Ministries.
www.enloeministries.org

Published By:
E M Publications
P.O. Box 780900
Wichita, KS 67278-0900

Printed in the United States of America

ISBN: 978-0-9794331-2-2

Scripture is taken from the King James
Version of the Bible.

First Edition.

Contents

Forward

By Tim Enloe

While studying at Central Bible College many years ago, I was assigned to read "The Real Faith" by Charles S. Price. I must admit that I was not too enthused about having to read another book—especially an old one—yet once the pages began turning, I was caught away into a new world of understanding. One after another my deepest questions about faith and healing were being answered so thoroughly and biblically.

"Why are so many not experiencing God's healing touch today?"

"Why does it seem so hard to work up enough faith for a miracle?"

"Why are the subjects of faith and healing so difficult to understand?"

"How can I be more effective in ministering healing to others?"

You may have similar questions to mine. I pray that you will share the enlightenment I received as Dr. Price, a renowned man of God, explains how simple it is to receive faith and healing from God, the source of every good and perfect gift.

Today so many misunderstand faith because it is often presented to be the product of a personal, mental pep-rally. Dr. Price will unload many common misconceptions and help you come to a new level of dependence on Christ—not your own ability to think positively.

If you are wounded because a minister or fellow believer told you the reason healing did not come is because of your imperfect faith, I pray that this book will provide answers to ease your mind.

If you are plagued with guilt or condemnation because you or someone you love has not experienced the healing needed, I pray that Dr. Price's words will be a healing balm to your spirit and lead you to a deeper walk with Christ.

With great joy, we are pleased to present the complete, original text of one of the greatest books on faith ever penned, "The Real Faith."

Introduction

Dr. Charles S. Price His Life, Ministry and Influence

By Tim Enloe

Standing before a silent crowd of thousands, the evangelist with a mild British accent dipped his index finger into the glass bowl of anointing oil. Touching the oil-covered fingertip to the forehead of the sick he prayed, "May the mercy of God and the love of our Lord Jesus Christ, and the power of His Holy Spirit—which are here now— enter your soul, your mind, and your body for healing. Amen."[i] The person receiving ministry then typically collapsed into the waiting arms of an altar attendant—apparently lost in another reality—as he or she was laid upon the floor.

This scene was commonplace in the ministry of Charles S. Price—one of the most noteworthy Pentecostal evangelists of the twentieth century.

Dr. Price, as his enthusiasts affectionately called him, had made a long personal journey from another continent, another belief system, and truly another way of life before he was catapulted in front of some of the largest evangelistic crowds of the era.

Early Life

Born in 1887, Charles Sydney Price was raised in Sheffield, England by his deeply religious father and stepmother; his birth mother passed away when he was only two. His photographic memory aided by his stepmother's encouragement toward education allowed young Charles to enter high school by age twelve.[ii]

After high school he served in the British Navy for two years.[iii] His parents made immense sacrifices to send young Charles to Wesley College, then to Oxford University for a total of two years studying law.[iv] After college, he was articled to a prominent Sheffield law firm and began to admire living the high life.

> While I loved my parents deeply, I foolishly began to believe that their outlook on life was old-fashioned and rather narrow. I had been caught in a social whirl and had become the friend of the sons of men, some of them titled [British nobility], who lived in a very different sphere from my simple and beautiful home surroundings.[v]

A series of rebellious decisions would eventually lead him to another continent to escape the past and try to find himself.

Departure From England

In September of 1906[vi], nineteen-year-old Charles left England for a fresh start in Canada. He searched diligently for work from Quebec to Winnipeg, going from one law firm to the next, but no one seemed to need a relatively inexperienced immigrant.

After much struggle, he ended up in Medicine Hat, Alberta at the home of long-standing friends of his parents; they helped young Charles get a job on the Canadian railroad. A few months later, Price felt a strange leading to go to Spokane, Washington and found himself leaving yet another country to find purpose and direction.

Immigration records show that he crossed the border on March 20, 1907—bound for Spokane—with $42 in his pocket.[vii] Some months after arriving in Spokane, he encountered an evangelistic service at the Free Methodist "Life Line Mission" that would restore his childhood faith and bring new direction to his life.

When Mr. Stayt gave his altar call, I sprang to my feet, squared my shoulders and marched down to the front....So that night I gave myself to God....It was a quiet, methodical, almost business-like proposition I made to the Lord; yet I meant it. I was sincere.[viii]

By the very next night Price was participating in Life Line's services, giving his conversion testimony. A short while later, the mission workers elected him to lead the service when the scheduled speaker did not arrive. With much fear, he preached his first gospel message and two men responded for salvation. Afterward, another attendee of the meeting introduced himself to Price as Dr. Henry I. Rasmus, the pastor of First Methodist of Spokane. Putting his arm around Price, he said, "My boy, God wants you. I believe he led me into this mission to speak to you....You are going to become a Methodist preacher."[ix] This was the beginning of Price's career as a clergyman.

Another significant event happened while at the Life Line Mission: he fell in love with one of the workers, Bessie Osborn, and they were married in late 1907.[x]

Journey Into Modernism

It appeared like Price had finally found what he was looking for—purpose, fulfillment, love and ministry—however, this new discovery was to be short-lived.

One of Price's friends had made a spiritual pilgrimage to the Azusa Street Revival in Los Angeles. Soon, several of the other mission workers were also baptized in the Holy Spirit, and Price could not help but notice the dramatic change in his friends' lives. He became convinced of the reality of the Pentecostal baptism and while en route to a tarrying meeting (to pray until he received the baptism in the Holy Spirit with speaking in tongues), he was intercepted by another minister who sternly warned him of the dangers of this new fanaticism. Price listened to the minister's anti-revival apologetic all afternoon and was finally convinced to stay away from the tarrying meeting and Pentecostalism in general.

Later in life, he frequently lamented his decision that day:

> That was the turning point in my life. With all my heart I believe that God had led me to Spokane so that I might step through the open door into the glorious experience that I am enjoying today, but I listened to the voice of a modernist and by my own act closed the door. Two roads were opened before me and I took the wrong one. I foolishly turned my back on the cross and started along the trail that led to the labyrinths of modernism...

> The conflict within my own breast was the age-old battle of reason against faith. How grieved and sorry I am today to have to record that reason won.[xi]

This decision plunged Price into Modernism, the liberal movement affecting Christianity in the early 1900s. He

12

quickly began to reason away his previous salvation experience, and his ministry from that point would be marked by the absence of altar calls and salvations for several years.

His first of seven[xii] Methodist pastorates was in Sedro-Wooley, Washington. He then went on to ministry in Anacortes before landing in Athol, Idaho. He was ordained by the Methodist Episcopal Church[xiii] and continued to pastor several churches in northern Idaho and eastern Washington.

Price's Modernistic theology continued to develop until he was called to task by his presiding elder for some of his teachings. This would be the inciting factor that led him to pastor more liberal Congregational churches for the next few years.

The Prices' first Congregational church was in Valdez, Alaska (1913-1915[xiv]). While there, he was naturalized as a U.S. citizen[xv] and was selected to serve as a member of the United States Alaskan Floating Court (the unique mobile court system for the lesser inhabited areas of Alaska). Once again he thrived on social standing and notoriety. His hunting expeditions, dog sledding, and photography of Alaskan life would later open doors for his blossoming oratorical skills.

Since his wife Bessie had been ill for the duration of their Alaska pastorate, the decision was made to relocate to a warmer climate. Bessie and the four children—Ethel, Marjorie, Vernon and Lucille—would go back to stay with her family in Spokane to recover while Charles headed for California in search of a new pastorate.[xvi] Valdez newspaper clippings tell of a packed out church listening to Price's "eloquent" farewell address.[xvii]

Soon after Charles Price landed in San Francisco, the First Congregational Church of Santa Rosa invited him to be their pastor, and Bessie and the children rejoined him in California. There from 1915-1917,[xviii] he climbed the local social ladder and quickly became a prominent public figure. In mid-1917,[xix] invitation was given to assume the pastorate of the sophisticated Calvary

Congregational Church in Oakland, and the Prices once again relocated. Charles Price became friends with the well-known pastor of Oakland's First Baptist Church, Dr. William Keeney Towner, and together they shared a private box in the T & D Theater in the city.[xx]

By this point, Price was deeply entrenched in Modernism and the social gospel. He led the church to install a white maple dance floor with the capacity of 1,500 and smoking lounges.[xxi] Price himself took up cigar and pipe smoking[xxii] and his messages were mainly on psychology and current issues. He would later recount,

> For sixteen years I never had a convert and for sixteen years I never gave an altar call…I used to love to rise in my pulpit and tell the folks of the theatres I had attended the past week, just to show how broad I was; and I belonged to almost every lodge and club that I could join.[xxiii] [xxiv]

His oratory skills soon opened even more prominent doors of opportunity; he was appointed to give four-minute persuasive speeches to sell war bonds for the government in theaters and shipyards. Receiving a Presidential commendation for this work and appointment to the U.S. Committee on Public Information, he would share the stage with many Hollywood celebrities during these many events.

His recognition as an articulate and entertaining speaker was rapidly increasing. It was no surprise when he received a letter from the Ellison-White Chautauqua System inviting him to be an entertainer for their programs. Resigning his pastorate in 1920,[xxv] he would tell of his adventures in Alaska and show his prized lantern slides as he entertained the crowds at Camp Curry in the Yosemite Valley (as a comedic entertainer during the summer and a lecturer during the winter; this would last for six consecutive seasons[xxvi]). Rev. and Mrs. Willard Peirce, early Pentecostal pioneers, would enjoy Price's comedy, impersonations, and poetry recitations while vacationing there in 1920.[xxvii]

The following year, he accepted the pastorate of the First Congregational Church in Lodi, California, where he would also continue Chautauqua lecturing on a part-time basis. Lodi is where his life's journey would take yet another turn—this time for the better.

Rededicates Life to Christ

In August of 1921,[xxviii] some of the Lodi church members told Price of an incredible revival happening in San Jose—replete with mass salvations, miraculous healings, and tongues speaking. He was immediately unimpressed and told them, "I can explain it all. It is metaphysical, psychological, nothing tangible."[xxix] Even so, Price had to admit "some of my best church members were getting inoculated."[xxx]

In an attempt to stop what he considered foolishness, Price decided to witness firsthand the San Jose revival being conducted by Aimee Semple McPherson. He planned on going as a skeptical observer, taking notes, and then dismantling the revival and the alleged miracles publicly in Sunday morning's sermon, but first he took out an ad in the local paper with his Sunday sermon topic, "Divine Healing Bubble Explodes."[xxxi]

Imagine his surprise when arriving in San Jose he saw the sign, "Aimee Semple McPherson; Auspices William Keeney Towner"![xxxii] His friend and theater partner from back in Oakland was sponsoring the fanaticism!

McPherson's tent was packed with about six thousand people, and many more crowded outside to hear her message. Price met an exuberant Towner in the aisle and listened as his old friend frankly told him, "Charlie, this is real. This little woman is right. This is the real gospel. I have been baptized with the Holy Ghost. It's genuine, I tell you. It is what you need."[xxxiii]

Price could only find an open seat in the "cripples" section and he later noted, "That is where I belonged."[xxxiv] He was surprised to find that Sister McPherson's theology was thoroughly biblical and convicting; so much so that hundreds responded for salvation after just one sermon. He noted to himself, "That woman has won more people to Jesus Christ in one fore-noon than you have gotten in fourteen years of your ministry."[xxxv]

That evening, he sat on the platform with the other ministers and though initially skeptical, became convinced of the reality of the healings he was witnessing. A blind person could now see; a man with crutches leapt from the platform in joy.[xxxvi] When Sister gave the invitation for salvation, Price raised his hand to respond. A fellow minister tapped him on the shoulder and said, "Charlie, don't you know she is calling for sinners?"[xxxvii] Price responded, "I know who she is calling for." [xxxviii] He was quick to respond to the altar and confirmed that he "walked out of that tent a new man"[xxxix] with a renewed commitment.

McPherson asked Price to testify and lead the singing the next day at the services. Willard Peirce was in attendance and turned to ask his wife why the song leader looked so familiar. She reminded her husband of their previous vacation to Yosemite Valley and the comedic entertainer from camp Curry; it was the same man![xl] The Peirces and Prices were to become dear friends in the years following. Willard and Christine Peirce hosted some of Price's mammoth campaigns in Toronto and were his last visitors before he passed away in 1947.[xli]

Needless to say, Price never preached the advertised sermon. In fact, it was much to the contrary. He was surprised when, after preaching an uncompromising gospel message, his church did not fire him. Instead over eighty people responded to the altars! Price had a dramatic change of heart that would remain for the rest of his life:

> In the course of a few short days not only outlook on life, my viewpoint, but my life itself had been transformed and changed. The burning, flaming fires of evangelism began to blaze in my heart. The thing that I desired

more than anything else in the world was to win souls for Jesus.[xlii]

This blazing fire in his heart would awaken a hunger that he had suppressed since his early days in Spokane; he was fourteen years late for a tarrying meeting!

Receives the Spirit Baptism

Sister Aimee conducted several services daily in the San Jose tent. Following the evening services, crowds as large as 600 would migrate to Dr. Towner's Baptist church for all-night tarrying meetings to receive the Spirit baptism.[xliii] Towner helped Price see the necessity of the Spirit's power in his life:

> Charles, you had better go all the way through. It is like trying to build a house without a hammer and saw—preaching without the Baptism of the Holy Ghost... Never mind your doubts, forget your dismay, you confessed to me there's a hunger in your heart and I advise you to seek the infilling of the Holy Ghost.[xliv]

After four nights of tarrying, God dealt with Price about his integrity, ambition and pride. He finally came to the place where he was no longer driven to pastor large, metropolitan churches, but was willing to pastor even a small mission not unlike the Life Line Mission he had previously attended. With all of the pride-breaking God was accomplishing in Price, he still was concerned about drawing attention to himself or being a spectacle, especially that he would be overcome by God's power and fall over in public:

> I looked around at the people that were prostrate under the power of God and I did not like that. I did not see the necessity for that and I said to myself, "why cannot God baptize a man with the Holy Ghost while he is kneeling down?" I asked a brother, I think it was Dr. Towner, "Brother, does everybody go down when they get the Baptism?" He said, "Well I did,

17

AND I HAVE AN IDEA YOU WILL." Well, that is all the comfort I got out of him.[xlv]

Price found an inconspicuous place to pray—behind a piano that had been crowded into a corner. At about 1:15 in the morning,[xlvi] Dr. Towner found Price still praying in secret behind the piano and convinced him to come out of hiding and pray with the others, "You have still got too much of this 'ministerial dignity' on your shoulders," he said.[xlvii]

Within just a few minutes of praying "in the open," Price suddenly felt the power of God coming upon him. He began to tremble and became aware that something else was happening, "I felt so light! Just like a feather. I was going up, and yet my eyes told me I was going down—the feeling was one of going up, but in reality I was just sinking to the floor."[xlviii]

The power of God continued to increase until:

A feeling of glory came through my body and I tried to say, "Praise the Lord" and I could not. I commenced to stammer and Dr. Towner commenced to shout and to praise the Lord and he said, "Praise Him" and I said, "Prai—praise—prai—." I could not…with stammering lips…I had them for just a moment or two and just then, suddenly, just as spontaneously and easily as water going over a fall I COMMENCED TO SPEAK IN ANOTHER TONGUE."[xlix]

This experience would dramatically change the course of his life and ministry; his church in Lodi would never be the same.

Soon, following Dr. Towner's model, Price's First Congregational Church of Lodi became the scene of all-night, Pentecostal tarrying meetings. Crowds would reach 1,000,[l] and the impact would be regional. Revival was shaking the once-liberal church! Within just a few months of his baptism in the Spirit, Price would report over 500 from the

Lodi church having the same experience.[li]

As a natural outgrowth of the revival, the church formed a gospel team of hundreds[lii] to minister in the community and in the surrounding region. Caravans of as many as 20 carloads of workers would go to nearby towns to hold evangelistic street meetings.[liii]

A seemingly serendipitous chain of events would launch Price from the Lodi church into international prominence and the most fruitful ministry he had ever witnessed.

Call to Evangelism

Aimee Semple McPherson had asked Price to travel with her evangelistic party to revivals in Canton, Ohio and Rochester, New York.[liv] The effectiveness of the McPherson campaigns—along with the amazing success of the Lodi church's traveling gospel team—stirred his heart for itinerant evangelism. All that was missing was confirmation from God.

After returning to Lodi from his easterly trip with the McPherson party, he spent several days in prayer and bewilderment. While things were going well at the church—and a larger sanctuary was under construction to house the increasing crowds—Price was still confused.

He took a train to Oakland to visit some friends and, while walking down the street, wandered into a restaurant. A man dining there called out to him saying, "My name is Miller. I am the pastor of the First Baptist Church of Ashland, Oregon. I believe you have come into this restaurant in answer to prayer."[lv]

Dr. B. C. Miller had come to California as a representative of the Ashland, Oregon churches to persuade Aimee Semple McPherson to hold a campaign there; McPherson was not able to do so, but recommended that Miller invite Price in her place.[lvi] Divine providence had spoken, and arrangements for the first Charles S. Price citywide evangelistic campaign were set in motion.

Catalyst of Revival

The Ashland campaign started on September 3, 1922[lvii] in the 5,000-seat Chautauqua lecture hall (the town's population at the time was also about 5,000[lviii]). By September 9th, crowds of over 3,000 would witness miracles at the first divine healing service.[lix] By September 22, the impact of the campaign would be in full swing as the building was filled and the local newspaper would read "Few Sinners in Ashland" as a subtitle on the main page.[lx]

The following scene is recorded in a secular newspaper about a healing service at Medford during this same series of revival meetings:

> The first 37 people who moved across the platform were so filled with the power of God that they had to be carried to their seats in the church. Out of 50 people prayed for, 47 fell under the power of God. The Lord was present in such a mighty way that twice Dr. Price collapsed and had to lay on the floor at one time to get control of himself. During the last half hour of the healing service, the evangelist was literally held up in the arms of two of the preachers. One deaf and dumb girl heard and spoke... one goiter melted away to such an extent that the preachers were crying "Look, look!" and some of the audience broke from their seats...it was a great night in Medford.[lxi]

Word of the revival in Oregon quickly spread, and pilgrims came from as far as British Columbia to experience the power of God, one of whom would open the doors to Canadian ministry for Dr. Price.

From his first meeting in Victoria, BC, the power of God only increased in the evangelistic campaigns. Deep conviction of sin and remarkable healings along with the curious sign of prostration during healing prayer attracted large crowds and surprisingly good favor. From West to East, Price would re-trace his earlier steps across Canada as a troubled young man. This time, however, he would bring the gospel to the largest arenas from Vancouver to Toronto, bringing hope and purpose to people who were lost.

In the Winnipeg campaign, a conservative Methodist pastor named D. N. Buntain was introduced to the Spirit baptism and joined the ranks of the Pentecostals; he later became the general superintendent of the Pentecostal Assemblies of Canada and father of the Pentecostal missionary statesman Mark Buntain.[lxii] In Edmonton, Alberta the 12,000-seat ice arena was filled to capacity, and some broke windows to climb into the building.[lxiii] There a young man, Lorne Fox, was healed of a terminal heart condition that had included 19 heart attacks, He would later carry on the campaign ministry of Dr. Price after his death.[lxiv]

Headlines touted: "300 Prostrate at Once After Anointing at Arena,"[lxv] "8,000 Present at Meeting of Faith Healing,"[lxvi] "Lame Arise from Chairs and Walk,"[lxvii] "Cripple Walks at Arena: Scores Go Down as if Before Machine Guns,"[lxviii] "Deaf and Dumb Converse After Evangelist Prays,"[lxix] and "Prayer Restores Sight."[lxx]

Minneapolis, St. Louis, Dallas, Seattle, Oklahoma City, Kansas City, Pittsburgh, Los Angeles and many other metropolitan areas would host huge Price campaigns. His meetings would also bear much fruit in smaller towns, such as Belleville, Illinois, where there were 10,000 conversions in ten days.[lxxi]

From 1922 to the late 1930s, Price's mammoth campaigns brought the Full Gospel's message and experience to the masses of the United States, Canada and Northern Europe; even the great Depression did not hinder his efforts. However, World War II brought fuel rationing and restricted travel, even blackouts; these factors greatly limited the possibility for mass meetings. During this period, Dr. Price would turn his effort to writing and meetings primarily in the populous region of Southern California where he called home.

In a 1940 Maywood, California tent meeting, a dairy farmer insistently approached Price to go to the hospital and pray for his dying sister. This young lady, Florence, had been in a car accident involving a paving truck—hot asphalt had spilled all over her body and covered her with third degree burns. Her pelvis was broken in seven places, and her leg had been torn loose from the socket. Dr. Price went to the hospital and prayed for Florence's healing—which God miraculously granted to the amazement of the hospital staff. This man, Demos Shakarian, became a close friend to Dr. Price, and they would meet weekly for lunch until Price's death in 1947.[lxxii]

Influence and Contribution

Demos Shakarian, founder of the Full Gospel Business Men's Fellowship International, was not the only prominent charismatic movement leader whom Price deeply influenced. In his 1922 Albany, Oregon campaign, strange circumstances brought a young girl from Concordia, Missouri to the meetings. There she witnessed Spirit baptism, divine healing, and prostration for the first time; this experience would significantly mark her life. Kathryn Kuhlman would become the leading proponent of these same three experiences in the 1960s and 1970s.[lxxiii]

Charles Price was one of the most prolific Pentecostal authors of his era, writing twenty-one books and editing his *Golden Grain* monthly periodical—of which he was the primary contributor—for twenty-one years. Of all his works, the book you are now holding, *The Real Faith* has had the broadest impact; it has been continuously in print since 1940. The thesis of *The Real Faith* is that faith is more than merely hoping or saying the right things (such as the positive confession movement would teach), but rather, a divinely imparted spiritual commodity that comes as you draw nearer to Christ; a sudden certainty that God alone can give.

Though Price's ministry was interdenominational, he found a special home in Assemblies of God circles. Serially preaching district camps in Oregon, Iowa, Minnesota, North Dakota, and Pennsylvania—to name only a few, he would also preach at the AG's biennial

General Council on occasion. He influenced and inspired a generation of young Pentecostal pastors to convincingly preach and boldly demonstrate the power of the gospel.

A host of postwar healing evangelists would devour his books and magazines to further their own ministries. T. L. Osborn would note that the *Golden Grain* was a lifeline during his early stint as a missionary in India.[lxxiv] Price's healing ministry would be a model that many would emulate.

Conclusion

Charles S. Price suffered heart problems for about three months prior to his death,[lxxv] and on March 8, 1947 he passed away—only two months shy of his 60th birthday. The funeral was conducted by two of his closest friends, Rev. Claire Britton of Alhambra, California and Rev. A. A. Wilson of Kansas City, Missouri. He was interred in Forest Lawn Memorial Park in Glendale, California[lxxvi]—not far from the grave of Aimee Semple McPherson.

Evangelists Hattie Hammond and Lorne Fox would fulfill Price's speaking engagements. His long-term assistant and governess to the children, Evelyn Carvell, would continue to publish the *Golden Grain* periodical for more than ten years. His writing ministry would continue to be promoted by his faithful daughter Marjorie until her death in 1994; the messages printed in his many books have proved to be his own written legacy.

This lost young man who made his long, personal journey from England to the United States via Canada—from rebellion to Modernism to Pentecost—had indeed found himself. From Sheffield, England to worldwide spiritual influence, his journey was complete.

Still today, the evangelist with a mildly British accent and a profound salvation/healing ministry is affecting many through his preserved teachings on the Holy Spirit, divine healing and other Pentecostal themes.

The Real Faith

1

In Which I Confess

FOR YEARS I have known something was wrong. What that something was I have now discovered, as the Holy Spirit Himself has unfolded before my bewildered eyes a vision of surpassing loveliness; and for the first time I have beheld new beauty and glories of the Lord in the heart of that grace we call FAITH. I call it a grace, because that is just what it is. In our blindness of heart and mind, we have taken faith out of the realm of the spiritual and, without realizing just what we were doing, have put it in the realm of the metaphysical. An army of emotions and desires has driven Faith from the chambers of the heart into the cold and unfruitful corridors of the mind.

Why have our prayers gone unanswered? Why are there so many sick, in spite of the fact that for them the so-called prayer of faith has been offered? Why are our churches filled with the lame and the halt, the deaf and the blind, who sit listening to sermons on divine healing that are true to the Word, and true to the promises of our Lord, and yet are not healed.

More than once I have gone home from some meeting with the shouts of victory ringing in my ears... but I have gone home to weep and cry, out of a disappointed heart, unto my Lord. The crowds were shouting because of some who were healed; but I was weeping because of those people who dragged their tired, sick bodies back to their homes— just as needy as they were before they came into the services.

Was there no balm in Gilead? Was there no compassion or sympathy in the heart of the Man with the nail prints in His hands? Why were some healed in such a miraculous way, and others dismissed with an appeal to keep on believing and return later, to go through the formula again?

> *In our blindness of heart, we have placed faith in the realm of the metaphysical.*

We must face facts. It is not pleasing to the Holy Spirit to dismiss the evident discrepancy between theology and experience with a shrug of the shoulders, and refuse to ask for light and guidance on this all-important problem.

Only the truth can make us free from the bondage of fears and doubts, and the discouragement that ultimately comes at the end of the road of disappointments. The only way to get the truth is to come in sincerity and absolute honesty of heart and mind to Jesus. Our Lord said that He Himself was the Truth, and as we open the door of the heart to Him we make possible the sweet revelations that only His presence can bring.

So I am going to be very, very frank. Sometimes, perhaps, almost painfully so. I cannot spread my heart out over these pages and do otherwise; for never before in my ministry as a writer have I been so stirred in my innermost being as I am now. This glorious and wonderful truth has flooded my soul, until it has lifted me in spirit to the gates of the glory world. I believe and pray that ere you finish these chapters, you too will see the gates of Grace swing open, and your feet will walk down the paths of Faith to the place where you will meet your Savior in the garden of answered prayer.

I come not as a dogmatist, wearing the robes of infallibility; neither come I as a wielder of the pen of sarcasm dipped in the ink of criticism; but rather as a grateful child of God, to whom the Holy Spirit has been giving Light on a subject which has been viewed through a glass darkly in the years that are past. But *now*, though the love of "The Giver Of Every Good And Perfect Gift,' there has come to me an understanding, in part at any rate, of the real and genuine meaning of that beautiful faith of which Jesus not only spoke, but imparts to men. *The revelation has answered my questions*. It has solved my problems. It has deepened my love for my Lord, and strengthened my surrender of heart and life to Him. It has revolutionized my healing ministry, for it has revealed to me the helplessness of self; and the need of the presence, the love, the grace, and the faith, of *Jesus*.

So I want to confess. I want to confess that my heart has been heavy, even when the crowds were shouting, singing, and declaring victory. I could see the miraculous cases of the healing touch of the hand of Jesus that were manifestations of His supernatural power. How glad I have been for them. They stand today as impregnable testimonies to the power of the Lord. They are unassailable fortresses, in the realm of experience, over which is flying the glorious banner of Truth.˙ There are thousands and thousands of these miracles; and they prove conclusively that Jesus is really the same yesterday, today, and forever. Not that we should rely upon experience to prove the Word, but it is blessed indeed when we can see manifestations of answered prayer. Yet, from those meetings, I have gone home with the faces of poor supplicating people haunting me. I have seen them do *their* best to rise from the wheel chair, only to sink back again in sorrow and disappointment. I have been moved by the groans, cries, and intercessions around altars, until they have lingered with me for days after the services were over.

You have also. In *your* church there is a multitude of sick and needy people. They love the Lord, they are consecrated to Him, yet there seems to be such need for a greater lifting of the physical burdens of life in answer to prayer. Ministers of the Gospel have taken me aside scores of times and told me of their discouragements because of their seeming inability to exercise *active* faith in God. If it were not for the fact that every once in a while some suffering soul reaches though and brings the glory down, many of these ministers would feel like running away when requests for prayer are sent to them. Not that these men are not God's men—they are! They are devoted to their calling and to the Lord, but they stand bewildered before what seems to be a contradiction between word and experience.

It does not seem quite right to sing, "Jesus never fails," and then watch the sick go out with their pains, their sicknesses and ailments, after the benediction. It is one thing to dismiss the suppliant with the words, "Only Believe;" but it is another thing entirely to dismiss that case from your thought and heart, if you are really sincerely honest before God. To testify to healing on the basis of faith or promise, before it has happened, is generally unwise, and always inexcusable, unless the faith is actually there. Even when it is there, it is better by far to be able to testify with the *double* voice one the articulate voice of praise and thanksgiving, and the other the inarticulate voice of the physical manifestation itself. Remember that faith—the weight of a grain of mustard seed—will do more than a ton of will, or a mind full of determination. Genuine faith can no more manifest itself without result, than the sunshine without light and heat.

Knowing this, and believing it to be true, what is it that we have been mistakenly calling faith, because real faith never fails to bring about the result? In my own heart, I am satisfied that many of God's children have failed to behold the difference between faith and belief. To believe *in* healing is one thing; but to have faith *for* it is altogether something else. That is why so many needy people, who believe, come to the Lord on the basis of His promises in the Word and *try* and *try* and *try* to affirm that they are healed.

OUR DIFFICULTY

Therein has been our difficulty. We have made faith a condition of mind, when it is a divinely imparted grace of the heart. Brethren, we have been wrong in our attitude and practice over and over again. When the golden sunlight of God's great grace and truth floods our hearts and minds, and when by the power of the blessed Holy Spirit we behold the provisions of His love; there will be an end to our struggling and striving, and these lives of ours will be wrapped around with the garments of His peace. In that happy hour, we shall come to the realization that we can receive faith only as He gives it. No longer will we foolishly attempt to struggle to believe. Instead of the storm, on the Galilee of life, there will be a sweet and a beautiful calm. The disciples could have worked themselves up into an emotional frenzy, trying to still the anger of the tempest. But three little words from Jesus and the wind drops from a scream to a whisper, and the sea whimpers for a moment like a crying child in its mother's arms and then settles down to sleep on the breast of nature. Three little words from Jesus and the winds and the seas obey Him! The tempest would have laughed in the face of the disciples—though they uttered a million words of commands and rebukes in the will to believe, for the tempest knew it was greater than they.

Three little words from Jesus—one touch from His hand divine—and more is accomplished in the time of a lightning flash than all our struggles and mental endeavors could work in a thousand years. *We have made it difficult, when He wanted to make it so easy.* How my heart has bled as I have seen some poor, needy soul struggling so very hard to exercise what he thought was faith when deep down in my heart I knew it did not come that way. Moreover, I knew faith did not operate in process or in results in the manner in which he had struggled so long in his yearning to obtain.

At moments like that it was so hard to say anything, for it meant the overthrow of established systems and methods. It meant the abolition of certain mani-festations that for years have been needlessly associated with the exercise of faith. It meant that, having arrived at the end of the road of honest endeavor without the thing for which we had prayed and tried and tried to receive, we would be forced to come to the conclusion that there was something wrong in our attitude of soul and mind, or else the victory would have been won.

Wherein have we been wrong? Why are there so many who stand bewildered

> *We have made it difficult when He wants to make it so easy.*

and perplexed in the midst of their own misgivings, until perhaps doubt has entered and the gates have quietly closed to the trysting place with Jesus, in the garden of the heart. I think I know the answer! I am sure in my own heart that I have discovered what has been wrong. I can see now where so many missed the way. The only thing to do is to ask the Spirit to lead us back to the fork in the road where, because of our blindness, we left the trail. Then once again can we walk on the King's Highway of grace and prove in heart and experience that the Book is true and that our Jesus never fails. Remember that! If there have been disappointments and failure, it has been on our part; and not the failure of Him who today is our advocate before the Father's throne.

30

2
Till All Our Struggles Cease

ONE OF THE chief difficulties is our failure to see that faith can be received *only* as it is imparted to the heart, by God Himself. Either you have faith, or you do not. You cannot manufacture it; you cannot work it up. You can believe a promise, and at the same time not have the faith to appropriate it. But we have formed the habit of trying to appropriate by *belief;* forgetting the while that *belief is a mental quality*, and that when we try to believe ourselves into an experience, we are getting into a metaphysical realm.

But faith is spiritual—warm and vital—it lives and throbs, and its power is irresistible, when it is imparted to the heart by the Lord. It is with the heart that man believes unto righteousness. Heart belief opens the door of communication between us and the Lord and a divinely imparted faith becomes possible.

Is it not a fact that with most of us our conception of Faith has resulted in our struggling in an attempt to believe? It may be that, with all our struggling, we have come at last to the place where we do believe; and then we have been bewildered by the fact that we did not receive the thing for which we prayed. We must discern that such belief is not necessarily what the inspired Word calls faith. In later chapters, we shall give you many scriptures that prove beyond the shadow of a doubt the truth of this alarming statement.

According to the Word of God, all we need is *faith* as a grain of mustard seed, and the things which the world calls incredible and impossible will be brought to pass. How many times during the meetings we have conducted have we seen the scripture stories of yesteryear enacted again before our eyes!

The seventeenth chapter of Matthew is a chapter of contrasts. It climbs to the heights, and then goes down to the depths. It talks of mustard seed and mountains of despair and transfiguration; but what a lesson the Holy Spirit would bring to you and me on this great subject of faith through its priceless words. Down from the mountaintop of transfiguration came our blessed Lord. Down from the gates of heaven itself, where the glory breezes kissed His cheek and the angels wrapped around His shoulders the robes that had been woven on the looms of light. Down from a place of holy communion and encouragement to the place of human defeat and perhaps despair; for at the foot of the Glory mountain was a valley, and through it wound a trail of human bewilderment. There was sickness there. A crushed and bleeding heart was there. A father who had met an obstacle that had crushed him in spirit and in heart was there. Preachers were there, too. They had gone through the formula. They had rebuked the devil. They had shouted and groaned just like we have done a hundred times, and yet the things for which they prayed had never

32

happened. Even as with you and me.

THEN JESUS SPOKE

Then Jesus spoke! O glorious words of omnipotence! Matchless words of authority divine! With Him there was no struggle. There was no groaning, and no battle that was fierce and long, to bring about the answer to a broken father's prayer. He spoke. The devil fled. A happy boy, cuddled in his father's arms, sobbed his gratitude to God. A happy father embraced his boy and looked with tear-stained eyes of love and adoration at the face of the Man before whom devils fled.

> *The least amount of faith is greater than the largest amount of the Devil's power.*

Then again Jesus spoke! In answer to their question regarding their defeat, he said: "Because of your unbelief: for verily I say unto you, If ye have faith as a grain of mustard seed, ye shall say unto this mountain, "Remove hence to yonder place;" and it shall remove; *and nothing shall be impossible unto you."* What a statement! All we need is faith as a grain of mustard seed and mountains will tremble in fear as we approach.

Do you realize what Jesus was saying? He declared that the *least* amount of faith that He could give was greater and mightier than the *largest* amount of the power of the devil. Here was a David and Goliath experience in the realm of the soul. A mustard seed went to battle against a mountain and slew it; but it had required the faith that He alone could impart as a gift.

Did those disciples believe? Yes they did. They believed in Jesus. They believed in His promises. They believed in divine healing, or never would they have held the healing meeting that day. Believing just exactly like you and I have believed in healing services and in our church meetings, they prayed and importuned; but nothing happened. What they needed, according to Jesus, was faith—not a carload of it, but just a little faith—as a grain of mustard seed. That would be enough! That would be all that was necessary; if it was really *faith*.

When a woman in one of my congregations one night told me that she had all the faith in the world for her healing, I regretted to have to tell her that if I had faith as a grain of mustard seed—just that much of my Master's faith—what greater miracles would have been wrought in the mighty name of Jesus that night!

Let us face the issue squarely. Let us with open, surrendered hearts ask the Holy Spirit to send forth the Light and Truth to lead us to that Holy Hill. Is it not evident that when we have prayed what we thought was the prayer of faith and nothing happened, it must be that what we thought was faith was not faith at all? Did Jesus say that faith, as a grain of mustard seed, would work some times and not at others? Did He declare that it would be operative on occasions and inoperative at other times? Read the text. His declaration was clear, concise, and plain. There was nothing ambiguous about it. It was a plain statement of fact from the lips and heart of the eternal God Himself; and who can speak with greater authority than He?

> *Faith is not intellectual, but spiritual.*

Whenever and wherever this *faith* is in operation, we shall no longer be standing around poor, sick folk hour after hour, rebuking, commanding, demanding, struggling, and pleading as in the days of yore. There may be a place for intercession, but it is not in the exercise of faith. Intercession and groaning of the heart may precede the operation of faith; *but when God's faith is imparted, the storm dies down and there is great calm and a deep settled peace in the soul.* The only sound will be the voice of thanksgiving and praise. The full realization—that it was not our ability to believe that made the sickness go, but rather that the faith which is of God was imparted—wilt steal over our soul, like a morning daybreak, to bid the night shadows flee away.

Then it is morning—glorious morning—in our soul. We can believe in the morning; we can love in the morning; we can have confidence in the morning; but only *God* can send the morning. Lie alone can make it. We can believe in healing; we can believe in our blessed Redeemer and His power to heal; but only He, the Lord Jesus Christ, can work the work that will lift us to the mountain peaks of Victory.

THE TRUE WAY

The mistake with many people has been that they have confused their own ability to believe for the faith that is of God. To sit down and repeat over and over, "I am healed—I am healed—I am healed" is not only unscriptural, but extremely dangerous spiritually. I admit that such a spiritually unsound procedure might help a few neurotics, but it would never remove the mountains of which the Master spoke. How well do I remember the crippled man in a wheel chair, whose case would best illustrate

scores of others whom we have contacted from time to time. Around him were grouped a dozen people who were doing everything in their power to get him out of that chair. There were prayers and tears mixed with commands and rebukes; and every sincere effort was being put forward to get him to walk.

When I talked with him quietly, he told me with such deep sincerity that he had been trying so hard to believe. He informed me that he had had lots of faith but now was bewildered and perplexed as to what to do. I soon discovered that he had been entirely wrong as to what faith really is. He had thought that he would be healed if only he *could believe that he was healed.* That was what he was struggling and trying to do. He believed the promises of the Word. He believed in the power of Jesus to accomplish the miracle. He believed so many, many things—wonderful and glorious to believe in these days of doubt and fear—but he was trying to do the impossible. *He was staking the working of the miracle on his ability to believe mentally that it was done.*

I told him the story of a visit I once made to the house where Jesus turned the water into wine. I told him of how the Holy Spirit spoke to this unworthy heart of mine as I stood before those pots. I asked him if he believed the Bible story of the miracle that the Master did in Cana of Galilee. He told me that he did. As my thoughts turned back to that afternoon in Cana, I felt the warm glow of the presence of the Holy Spirit. This is the lesson I received that day. Though the mother of Jesus, as well as the disciples, was there, would that water have turned into wine if they had merely believed that it was wine? It required the command that left the lips divine! It required the touch of the hand of God Himself. They could fill the pots with water; they could fill them to the brim. They could carry them to the appointed place. They could do the things He told them to do; for *He never asks men to do the impossible. That power He reserves for Himself.*

> *He never asks men to do the impossible; that power He reserves for Himself.*

All things are possible *with God.* But Mark (9:23) tells us, "If thou canst believe, all things are possible to him that believeth." The belief that Jesus is speaking of here *is not head belief or mental acquiescence, but* that heart belief which is *faith.* This is proved by the account that Matthew gives of the story of the lunatic boy, to which we have already referred. In the account by Matthew, Jesus said, "If ye have faith as a grain of mustard seed;" while in the narrative recorded by Mark, "If ye believe." So the "belief" of Mark and the "faith" of Matthew are identical. That is my point. That is what the Spirit of God has been causing my poor eyes to behold *that faith is not intellectual, but spiritual.* It is primarily of heart—not of mind. Genuine, scriptural faith is not *our ability* to "count it done," but is the deep consciousness divinely imparted to the heart of man that *it is done.* It is the faith that only God can give. So I told my story to the old man in the wheel chair. Did you ever see a flower open to the smile and kiss of the morning sun? I saw one that day, as I looked into the face of the dear old man. Home he went to patiently wait until some angel voice would whisper in his soul the news that Jesus of Nazareth was passing by on the Jericho Road of his life.

A few nights later he was back in his wheel chair. I met him. "I am going to walk tonight," he declared. His eyes were alight with something I knew was faith. "How do you know it?" I asked him. "It is so quiet and peaceful in my soul; I am so happy in the consciousness of His presence, that all I need now is to obey His word and be anointed in His blessed name." There was no struggle; not even intercession, for that had gone before. There is no need of the darkness, when the sun has come up over the hill; no need for the struggle between darkness and light, that we call the morning twilight, after the rays of sunshine have kissed the earth! Out of his wheel chair he got and walked the length of the altar; then down on his knees in adoration, praise and worship, to pour out his grateful heart in thanks-

giving for the heart belief, or faith, that comes only from God.

THE MASTER'S VISIT

The postman has just been to my door. He left a letter that I want you to share with me. It is the story of a woman who was crippled beyond any I have ever seen in the many years I have presented my Lord as the Savior of the soul and the Healer of the body. When first I saw her, she begged piteously for prayer. She asked me to heal her. I could not, and I knew it. I might have gone through a series of commands, rebukes and pleadings, but I did not. I was just a disciple at the foot of the mountain; and I knew that we both needed our Lord to come down. I believed in Jesus, and His power to raise the fallen. I believed His promise, and I stood on His word. But as I looked into the face of a woman who had crawled on her hands for ten years, and who was helpless from the waist down, my heart told me that I needed more than just to believe she was healed. I needed the impartation of that faith which supercedes reason; I needed that spiritual quality of heart belief that no mental affirmations of mind could ever bring about. I knew that was what she needed too. So I pleaded with her to contact Jesus. I begged her to wait patiently for the Lord. Her hour would come. I felt it in my heart. I knew that Jesus never fails. But, oh how many times, we prevent His working by our foolish endeavors to do what He alone has power to accomplish. So day after day her husband and friends carried her to the meetings. Day after day she sought the face of the Lord. Night after night they picked up her helpless body and placed it before the old wooden bench where prayer was wont to be made. The days passed. In spirit she climbed the temple steps into the tabernacle of the Lord. She passed by the altars of surrender and sacrifice, and one night she entered into the Holy of Holies. What a night! It was Sunday. Healing was not on the program that had been printed by human hands. But God works wonders when Jesus of Nazareth passes by; and the Holy Spirit can make us rise above our forms, rituals and plans.

> *Her shriveled limbs grew to normal size faster than it takes to tell it.*

A beautiful spirit pervaded that Sunday evening service. Down at the altar, where she had been carried by her husband, she reclined to pray, for she could not kneel. Then Jesus came. He gave her a vision of Himself. She saw Him at the end of a road. He smiled. She was conscious of faith flowing like a river across the fields of her heart. Before it happened, she knew it! How, or why, she could not tell; but she knew that there had been a divine infusion of the Faith that is the Faith of the Son of God. At that very moment, the Savior imparted His Faith to my heart too. I turned to the Methodist minister on the platform and said, "Tonight we shall see the glory of the Lord." We did. As the hand of the Lord was laid upon her, she straightened out. Her shriveled limbs *grew* to normal size faster than it takes to tell it. She stood to her feet! She walked! No need to be carried now, except in the loving arms of Jesus. Down to the foot of the cross streamed sinners to seek a Savior! The building rang with the praises that come from happy hearts, and the rafters resounded with the message:

"Only Jesus, only Jesus,
Only He can satisfy.
Every burden becomes a blessing,
When I know my Lord is nigh."

ONLY JESUS

The reason for telling this story is that I want you to see the difference between human effort to believe, and the faith that is the gift of God. How much better, and more scriptural, it is to wait until Jesus of Nazareth passes by and speaks the word of faith to the needy heart, than to mistake our *belief in healing* for the *faith* which He alone can give.

Frankly, the day they first brought that poor, helpless woman for prayer, I was aware of three things. I knew she did not have *faith;* I knew I did not have *the faith;* and I knew that only Jesus had. So quite evidently our mission was to draw close to Jesus. It is our privilege to take our troubles and our cares to Him in prayer; and within our heritage is the right to draw apart from the world into the sacred place of communion, where heaven comes down—our souls to greet—and glory crowns the Mercy Seat.

That is what we did! We could have set our minds and our wills to work right then and there. We could have commanded, exhorted and entreated; and she could have struggled to rise, as others have done, *in the Power of will* instead of *in faith.* But no, there is a better and sweeter way. It is God's way! It is the Bible way. It was a long way for the nobleman to walk from Capernaum to Cana; but after he met Jesus, he never regretted the Journey. It may be that the trail will be steep over consecration mountain and through the valley of the yielded heart; but hope will give strength to our feet and, as we walk with Jesus in the way, the toils of the road will seem nothing; for He and He alone is the giver and imparter of that faith which is able to remove mountains.

I should like to share with you our sister's letter:

October 12, 1940
Laurel, Ontario

Dear Brother Price:

Christian greetings!

Oh, hallelujah, the joy bells are ringing in my heart because of Jesus! As the time draws near to another anniversary of the great miracle Performed upon my body, the thoughts and the warmth of my husband's heart and mine, go out to you in a very special way. Thank God, the blessed Christ came to us and manifested His Power and presence so Preciously to us, that evening, October 19, 1924.

What good measure He gave us! He saved my soul as well as healed my body, using you as His disciple. Truly I was in a pitiful condition, was I not, Brother Price? I was in great need both spiritually and physically. Spiritually, I thought I was saved, but was really sort of on the fence, having too much of the Lord to enjoy the world, and too much of the world to have real joy in the Lord.

Through your preaching the full gospel, the real joy of the Lord came into my heart, also my husband's to abide—with the assurance that our many sins were washed away in Jesus' cleansing blood. Physically—well, you pretty well know my condition in that respect, as you could see for yourself my helplessness when I was taken into your meetings, not being able to walk or stand, or even let my feet rest on the floor in the usual way when sitting in my chair.

Ten long years of helplessness, being carried in the arms of my faithful husband, with continual suffering; and then, Jesus again walked the Jericho Road, and came my way in your meetings. Oh yes, you have heard me tell of it many times, but I want to tell it to you yet again. The story never becomes stale to my husband or me, because you see it is Jesus. Dear Jesus! My heart overflows as I talk to you of it, and the tears are flowing too, for Jesus' love melts me down in praise and thankfulness before Him. Yes, Jesus heals sick bodies today! Keep on telling the good news, Brother Price, for there are so many sick and afflicted ones all about us. God's word tells us that Jesus healed the lame, the blind, the lepers, and all manner of diseases, when He walked this earth many years ago, and we do know that He does the very same in the days in which we live. His flower has not lessened. Those bleeding, healing stripes He bore at Calvary are just as efficacious now as then, Thank God.

Saturday, October 19, 1924, Jesus put me upon my helpless feet and enabled me to walk without an ache or a pain; and sent me on my way rejoicing, and truly my husband and I have been rejoicing ever since—in Jesus! Sixteen years of health, strength and activity. I have had some real tests in my body during those years, broken bones and different trials of faith, but I want to tell you once again, even though you so well know it, the Promises of God hold fast and sure. Our God gets all the glory, for neither my husband nor I have ever used the slightest remedy of any kind since Jesus so undertook for us at Paris, where we found the great Healer in those gospel meetings.

In thankfulness and praise to Jesus, we again wish to thank you, Brother Price, for the part you had in the great work. Like Paul, you were not disobedient to the heavenly vision, for you did not compromise in any way, but declared the whole truth, not leaving out that Jesus heals the sick today. My husband and I are so well in body, all glory and praise to Jesus our physician. Never any need for pills or liniment flaw; the promises are sufficient. Hallelujah! Jesus never, never fails.

We continue to Pray for you. May you ever be guided by the Holy Spirit, and anointed from above for even greater service than in Past years, to proclaim the unsearchable riches of Christ. How the Holy Spirit warms me as I write and the power of God thrills and fills me. Hallelujah! Jesus lives! How do we know? Thank God, because He lives within.

Cordial Christian love to you all, from your ever thankful friends in Jesus,

Brother and Sister Johnson

3
The Better Road

I BELIEVE THERE is a difference between the *faith* of the Old Testament under law and the *faith* of the New Testament under grace. The key word of Paul's epistle to the Hebrews is "better," and this is particularly interesting in the light of the fifth chapter of this remarkable letter. He is trying to get them to see the truth of Christianity by contrast. He does not abrogate the past, but shows them that Christianity grew out of Judaism just as the flower grows out of the root.

Hidden away in the ritual of the root was the color, the fragrance, and the beauty of the flower of grace that was to come later. Was not the flower better than the root? Was not the end better than the beginning? Was not the blood of Christ better than the blood of the lamb on Jewish altars slain? Was not Jesus better than the angels who had visited their fathers from time to time in memorable days of their national history? Was not the voice of God's Son better than the voice of the prophets? This then was the heartthrob of the Epistle. When he comes to the faith chapter, is there any reason for his departure from the purpose of the letter, and the motive of the epistle? I think not. The theme is still better, and the purpose is to show the beauty of the faith of Jesus in comparison to those works and words of the patriarchs and prophets that were counted unto them as faith. It was the faith of that day. It was the faith for that time.

Remember that Paul closes that faith chapter with the words, "God having provided some *better* thing for us, that they without us should not be made perfect." In other words, the acts and testimonies of the ancients were held up like pictures in a gallery for the Christian Jews to behold and admire. There was the story of Abel and Enoch. Noah, Abraham, Sara, Isaac and Jacob were framed in a picture of obedience to the divine word. Then there came Moses and Joshua, followed by a grand parade of the illustrious of the days of old, before Jesus was born in the stable of Bethlehem. But Jesus was born now— and nowhere in the entire epistle does Paul tell them, or us, that *our faith today* should be limited in its pattern, working, or operation to the faith of our fathers. *Instead, he tells of something better.* He introduces the flower that has grown out of the root.

Faith in the old days was manifested by word and deed in obedience to command. But there remains more. The word and deed are only a part, and a small one at that, of what the New Testament teaches us that faith really is. Of course, there will be work, and there will be testimony. But that alone is not faith. Not New Testament faith, at any rate!

In this connection, it is interesting to note that if you turn back to the Old Testament account of the lives of the men and women introduced in the eleventh chapter of Hebrews, the word *faith* is *never mentioned* in connection with their lives at all. The word faith occurs in the Old Testament only twice, and in one of those instances it is prophetic and in the other is used in a negative way regarding the unbelief of a wicked generation. The two passages are Deuteronomy 32:20 and Habakkuk 2:4. So we must come then to the unmistakable conclusion that Paul is not holding up the lives of these illustrious Patriarchs as a pattern for them to follow, but rather as the excellent beginning in God's will of some thing more wonderful which they were to discover in Jesus. *The faith they were to possess was all their fathers had and more.*

Seeing that they were surrounded by such a great cloud of witnesses, they too were to lay aside weights and sins and run with patience the *new* race which was set before them. They were to do what? Look to Jesus who was the *Author and Finisher of their faith.* If He was the Author and the Finisher of their faith, and the faith of Paul, then He is the Author and Finisher of my faith too. In other words, all true faith begins and ends in Him. It does not say that He is the Author and the Finisher of *His faith alone,* but it states that He is the Author and Finisher of *my faith* and of yours.

FAITH AND PRESUMPTION

There is nothing before the Alpha and nothing after the Omega. He begins it, and it begins in Him. He ends it and it ends in Him. When I want it, I must seek His face! I cannot get it anywhere else, but from that matchless One of whom it is said, He is the Author and the Finisher of our faith. Not of His alone but of y*ours and mine.* Have we made the mistake, after looking at the eleventh chapter of Hebrews and *seeing what they did then,* of rolling up our sleeves to show and prove our faith by what we do? Have you ever done that? If you have, then you have stood in bewilderment at what seemed to be unanswered prayer and the inoperative power of what you thought was faith! Remember that faith acts, but the act comes from the faith, rather

> *All true faith begins and ends in Him.*

than faith from the act. That is why it is very easy to step over the borderline from the Faith God imparts into the realm of presumption. This was illustrated to me in a very clear and wonderful way some time ago.

In Victoria, B. C., some years ago, I was entering the Metropolitan Methodist Church in company with a few ministers. At the door of the edifice we saw a kindly old lady being taken out of a truck in a wheel chair. I raised my hat and gave her a "God bless you." Tears welled up in her eyes as she replied, "He has been blessing me, Dr. Price. He is so kind and gracious, and I can feel His presence now." "Have you come for healing?" I inquired. "Yes, I have," she replied, "and praise His name, I know the waters are troubled." Just then the truck driver leaned over and said, "Shall I come back, lady, to take you home after the service?" She had traveled a good many miles, and the only way to get her home in a wheel chair was by truck, for the chair was too large for an automobile. She hesitated. Then a light came over her face as she replied, "No, I am not going to need a truck. I will leave my wheel chair behind and go home on the train." The driver scratched his bewildered head and grinned at what he thought was a foolish woman. Away he drove. And she did not need him! She went to her house rejoicing, and she went on the train!

I told that story in a meeting I conducted in the Middle West. The next day a lady sent a message that she would like to see me for a moment in her cottage. I found her lying on a couch with a group of people around her who were singing a hymn. She looked up at me and said, Brother Price, I have sent the wheel chair home." She waited for a shout from me. None came. Instead my heart fell. There was no faith and I knew it. She discerned I did not enthuse over her act, so she turned away from me and said, "If God can do it for one woman, He can do it for another."

When I left the building that night she was again the center of a group who were insisting that she arise and walk; but she went away sorrowful. Of her the

Lord could say, "There is one thing thou lackest." The two acts were just the same. Two wheel chairs were sent home. In one case it was faith; and *in the other it was presumption.* In New Testament faith, the act can be born of faith; but faith cannot be born of the act. The act can come from faith, but the faith must come from God.

This, then, is the *better* way of Paul's epistle to the Hebrews. This is the purpose and the motive back of what we call the Faith Chapter of the Book. Have you not stood in amazement before the unfolding benevolence and generosity of the Lord? Do you not know that no good thing will He withhold from them that walk uprightly? Have you a need? Take it to Jesus. Have you a problem? Lay it at the Master's feet. Begin to trust Him, and as you give Him your confidence and trust, you will find His Faith will become operative in you. Why play with the teacup of our struggles and endeavors when His faith is as boundless as the ocean?

He is no respecter of persons. He loves the weakest and the simplest of us all, but we become so important in our own eyes and so proud of our spiritual accomplishments that our testimonies display only the righteousness that is vainly of self. He looks at it—the righteousness that is filthy rags! We need to come in *the guileless spirit of little children*: come with the bells of love pealing in the belfry of our hearts! It is useless to wait until we feel we are worthy, for that we will never be. Come as a little child to the One who in the days of old set a little one in the midst of them and said to the Pharisees, "Except...ye become as little children, ye shall not enter into the Kingdom of Heaven."

Steal away softly to Jesus. In this day of

> *As you give Him your confidence and trust, you will find His Faith will become operative in you.*

grace, the faith for the Christian can be found only in Christ; but in our blessed Lord you will find sufficient for all your need. What Noah had was good, but what we have is better. Noah had God's Word, but we have God's Son. Noah built on God's Word, but our foundation is Jesus Himself. So we find it in the whole of that remarkable chapter: a recitation of God's glory manifest in the acts of men who believed God and who walked the walk of obedience with Him. One of them, named Enoch, went for a walk with Him one day and forgot to come back. When the faith that is of God came to earth in the form of the Son of God, Paul was constrained to say to the Hebrews, "That was the old faith, but here *is* the new. That was the good way, but this is the better."

A STORY OF MULLER

Christ was to be all in all. And the love of the Father's heart is shown in the fact that He is not only able, but _willing_ to meet our every need.

I have been reading the life of George Muller. Pastor Charles Parsons tells of an experience with Muller in the following words:

A warm summer day found me slowly walking up the shady groves of Ashley Hill, Bristol. At the top there met my gaze the immense buildings which shelter over two thousand orphans, built by a man who has given the world the most striking object lesson in faith it has ever seen. The first house is on the right, and here, among his own People, in Plain, unpretentious apartments, lives a saintly Patriarch, George Muller. Passing through the lodge gate, I paused a moment to look at House No. 3 before me, only one of the five erected at a cost of $600,000.

The bell is answered by an orphan, who conducts me up a lofty stone staircase, and into one of the private rooms of the venerable founder. Mr. Muller has attained the remarkable age of ninety-two. As I stand in his presence, veneration fills my mind. "Thou shalt rise up before the hoary head, and honor the face of the old man" (Leviticus 19:32). He received me with a cordial handshake, and bade me welcome, it is something to see a man by whom God has accomplished a mighty work; it is more to hear the tones of his voice; far more than either to be brought into immediate contact with his spirit, and feel the warm breath of his soul

48

breathed into one's own. The communion of that hour will be forever graven on my memory.

"I have read your life, Mr. Muller, and noticed how greatly, at times, your faith has been tried. Is it with you now as formerly?" Most of the time he leaned forward, his gaze directed on the floor. But now he sat erect and looked for several moments in my face, with an earnestness that seemed to penetrate my very soul. There was grandeur and majesty about those undimmed eyes, so accustomed to spiritual visions and to looking into the deep things of God. I do not know whether the question seemed a sordid one, or whether it touched a lingering remnant of the old self to which he alludes in his discourses. Anyhow, there was no shadow of doubt that it roused his whole being.

After a brief pause, during which his face was a sermon, and the depths of his clear eyes flashed fire, he unbuttoned his coat, and drew from his pocket an old-fashioned purse, with rings in the middle, separating the character of the coins. He placed it in my hands, saying, "All I am possessed of is in that purse—every penny! Save for myself? Never! When money is sent to me for my own use, I pass it on to God. As much as £1,000 has thus been sent at one time; but I do not regard these gifts as belonging to me; they belong to Him, whose I am, and whom I serve. Save for myself? I dare not; it would dishonor my loving, gracious, all bountiful Father."

> *There is the unchanging promise of Jehovah, and on that I rest.*

"The great point is never to give up until the answer comes. I have been praying for fifty-two years, every day, for two men, sons of a friend of my youth. They are not converted yet, but will be! How can it be otherwise? There is the unchanging promise of Jehovah, and on that I rest. The great fault of the children of God is, they do not continue in prayer; they do not persevere. If they desire anything for God's glory, they should pray until they get it. Oh, how good, kind, gracious and condescending is the One with whom we have to do! He has given me, unworthy as I am, immeasurably above all I had asked or thought! I am only a poor frail, sinful man; but He has heard my Prayers tens of thousands of times, and used me as the means of bringing tens of thousands into the way of Truth. I say tens of thousands in this and other lands. These unworthy lips have proclaimed salvation to great multitudes, and *very many have believed unto eternal life."*

Thus spake George Muller. Thus spake a man of our times, for I was in Bristol as a boy while Muller was yet alive. Thus spake a man who had learned the lesson that waters come from the fountain and that flowers come from the root. He had learned that the faith of God comes only from God and that nowhere else could it be found. He learned that He who was so free in the grace of giving would teach *His* disciples how to be efficient in the grace of receiving. When he needed money, he went not to the man who had *it*, but to the Christ who had the power to speak to the heart of the man who had it. His faith came because of his daily, vital contact with his Lord; and being in the will of God, he was given more than enough for every need.

Men used to call him "the nineteenth century apostle of faith." I suppose he must have heard that said about himself. I wonder if he ever read the eleventh chapter Of Hebrews. I wonder if he ever became conscious of the fact that men were adding his name to the roll of the heroes of faith. If he did, I think he must have smiled when he came to the last verse of that eleventh chapter of Hebrews and read, "God having provided something *better* for us." And he *must* have found what that better was when only two short scripture verses away he found the words, "Looking unto Jesus, the author and finisher of *our* faith."

So go to Jesus now. Learn to trust Him, that He might impart His faith! Acquaint Him with your need. Tell Him of your sorrows. Then, in the sanctuary of His presence, you will find rest and freedom from the noise and worries which beset you from without and within.

And His that gentle voice we hear,
Soft as the breath of even,
That checks each thought, that calms each fear,
And speaks to us of Heaven.

4
The Origins of Faith

I HAVE A very decided dislike for negative preaching and writing. It is not sufficient for a speaker or author to discuss the disease, but to satisfy my soul and mind, he must give me the cure. It is easy to point out what is wrong, but I want to know what is right. Sometimes that is a little more difficult than one would suppose. However, when at last honest mistakes have been rectified, and we are back on the paths of truth, it may be that in the providence of God the wrong trail will have left us a heritage of blessing.

Many years ago I was on one of my periodic visits to the mountain ranges that border on the rocky coasts of Alaska. A visitor to this land of the Great White Silence had been lost, and I had told him of the trail that would take him back to a valley where he could get his bearings. After a lapse of two hours he was back at my camp. He told me he was confused and completely turned around; and asked me if I would kindly travel with him until he was sure of his direction. I did, for it is a dangerous place in which to wander alone, unless one has a knowledge of the country and its trails. Weeks later I received a letter from the grateful fellow, in which he said among other things, "To know you are on the right road is a fine thing; but to return to it, after being on the wrong one, multiplies its blessing."

How true! It is after the rain that we appreciate the bursting buds and delicate greens of the early spring. After the storm clouds we appreciate the calm of a sky-blue day. If through these pages I can lead those dear children of God, who have not seen the full fruit of the victory of faith, back to the clear teach-ing of the Book and to ultimate victory, then this heart of mine will be happy and these pages, written in prayer, will not fail in their mission.

> *You cannot generate, work up or manufacture faith; it is imparted and infused by God alone.*

The thing above all else I want you to see is that you cannot generate it; you cannot work it up; you cannot manufacture it. It is imparted and infused by God Himself. You cannot sit in your homes and struggle to have faith, and affirm that something *is;* nor can you turn your hope and desire into faith by your own power. The only place you can get it is from the Lord, for the Word clearly and distinctly states that faith is one of two things. It is either a gift of God, or it is a fruit of the Spirit.

We are told in Paul's Epistle to the Corinthians, "Now abideth faith, hope, and love; but the greatest of these is love." While love might be the greatest, it certainly is not the first. It must be preceded by faith. Look out of your window at yonder tree. What a thing of symmetry and loveliness it is! Only God can make a tree. There is beauty in its twisted branches. There is loveliness in its trembling leaves. Every leaf is a little world unto itself, with its tiny veins carrying the life that God supplies, which gives it all it possesses in its native realm. Yet there is something back of the tree. Beneath the surface of the ground there is a great system of roots hidden away. You never behold them; yet without them the tree would die. It would have no life at all.

FAITH IS THE LIFE

The roots are ugly and hard in comparison to the beautiful greenery above the ground. Yet the greenery is there partly because of those roots. Now, let us call the top of the tree "Love." You can see it. You can contact it. You can enjoy its fragrance. You behold its beauty. It is there because of something that is back of it—something hidden away that causes it. That something is the roots. Now you expect me to say that those roots are the roots of faith.

No! *Faith is the life that flows into the roots.* It is that mystical quality that only God can produce and give. There are roots you could plant which will never, never grow. You, yourself, and your inner nature are those roots. Your senses, your avenues of approach to the expressions of life itself are buried below the surface where people cannot see them. All the world beholds is what you produce and not you yourself. What did Jesus mean when He said, "By their fruit ye shall know them?" Ye shall know *them.* The fruit produced is an index to what the tree really is.

Let me repeat. The roots of the tree are not faith. The roots do not produce the life, but the life produces the roots. *It is the life that is faith.* It is that wonderful and glorious quality which is a gift of the divine heart, and which sustains us. This life, or faith, will be manifest to the world by the fruit we bear; by the arms of love outstretched; by the things of grace and beauty which through God are manifested day by day on the tree of our lives.

How foolish it would be for that tree to

struggle in an attempt to create the life that flows into it. It need not struggle. All it needs to do is to function in obedience to the laws divine. As the life is there, it simply manifests that life in the fruit it bears, and the beauty with which it endows the world. So it is with faith. Love may be the greatest thing in the world, but faith must of necessity be the first. Without faith it is impossible to please God. But you tell me that *you* have faith. I ask you where you got it. I pick a rosy apple from a tree. I hear it testify from the core of its little apple heart. It tells me it has rosy cheeks. It whispers in my ear that it is so very good to the taste. It invites me to taste its flavor. It testifies that it has so many noble and beautiful qualities. Then I ask it where it got them all. From the branch? The shelter of the leaves, the rain and the sun? Yes, all true; but I knew that way down in the hidden system, which you can not see, the roots were receiving something from God that no tree on the

> *Love may be the greatest thing in the world, but faith must of necessity be the first.*

face of the earth has ever been able to produce of itself!

THE ATHEIST AND GOD

Some time ago an atheist sat in a meeting I was conducting. He was extremely hard and cynical. He lived alone in the room of a hotel, and his solitude had only added to his hard, critical, unbelieving nature. I preached that night on the subject "Comprehending the Incomprehensible." I declared that it was possible to believe the unbelievable; to know the love of God that passeth knowledge.

The following morning he came to my room and asked for an interview. He was rather argumentative and I told him, while I did not have time for argument, I would be glad to answer any sincere, honest question that he might put before me. He said, "I have no faith whatever. I do not believe the Bible, and I do not know if there be a God. I do see a law of order in nature and the universe, but what causes it, or where it came from, I do not know. Now, Dr. Price, your sermon last night was a challenge to my thinking. What I want to know is this: How can a man spend a dollar when he does not have one? How can you drive a car when you do not possess one? How can you believe when you have no belief? How can God expect a man to exercise faith when he does not have any (assuming there is a God)? Where is there justice in a set-up like that?"

"Are you an honest man, and do you want to know the truth?" "What is truth?" was the reply. "'What brand of it do you mean? I have never been able to find it, although I have spent a lifetime in search of it."

On the wall of my apartment was hanging a picture of Jesus in the Garden of Gethsemane. His hands were clasped and His eyes were raised toward heaven in prayer. I walked over to that picture and looked at it for a moment or two

without speaking. I intuitively knew he would be looking at that picture too. When at last I turned to face him, I said, "He is Truth. He is the Way. He is your Life and Faith. He has in abundance what you say you do not have. You have been trying to get it out of mind, thought, and intellect. He can put it there, as the river of His grace flows though your heart. That is why He came. He came to make men free; free from doubts like yours; free from fears and misgivings; free from unbelief and free from sin..."

"Sounds like a fairy story to me," he interrupted. "Fine if you can believe it, but how can man or God expect a man to believe what he can not believe?"

He went away. A week later he came to me and offered his hand. When I looked at his face, I knew the miracle had happened. Into his heart there had come not only the conscious knowledge of sins forgiven, but a manifestation of the sweetness and love of God which had made him a new creation in Christ Jesus. As in the millennium, instead of the briar shall come up the myrtle tree, so in this man's life there had sprung up the evidence of the indwelling presence of God.

"Do you know what happened?" he said. "I told the Lord to manifest Himself, *if He was there.* I asked Him to do something that would reveal His presence, *if He was there at all.* I became conscious that He was near me. I realized *there was* a God—that there was a soul to save. I did not understand it with my mind, but I knew it in my heart. Then I told Him I had no faith to believe, so *He gave me His faith,* and I believed. The work was done."

> *I told God that I had no faith to believe—so He gave me His faith—and I believed. The work was done.*

Why not? That is God's way of salvation. "As many as received Him, to them gave He power to become the Sons of God, even to them that believe on His name." When I give an altar call, I invite *every* man, and *every* woman, to surrender his heart and life to Christ.

If we are saved by Faith, how do I know that all can have the faith to receive? How do I know that *every one* whom I invite can find eternal life? Some might have faith, and others be entirely devoid of it. The fact that people *believe what you say* does not mean that they have the faith to translate that belief, or even heart hunger, into an experimental knowledge of sins forgiven.

Nevertheless, I cry, "Whosoever will may come," because I know that He will *impart the faith which is needful* to every sincere heart. I have quoted the twelfth verse of the first chapter of John: "But as many as received Him, to them gave He power to become the Sons of God, even to them that believe on His name." Let me quote the next one. Thus does it read: "Who were born (that is, born again) not of blood, nor of the *will of the flesh, nor of the will of man*, but of God." The same Holy Ghost who convicts the sinner of his sin will see to it that as the sinner was given enough conviction to convince him of his sin, so he will now be given faith enough to convince him of his salvation. But no man *in himself* possesses that faith. Are we not told "By grace are ye saved, through *faith; and that not of yourselves; it is the gift of God."* Poor, wretched, miserable, ignorant, unbelieving humanity could *never* grow or develop in such corrupt hearts of unbelief faith enough to believe in a Savior, let alone receive Him. So the Holy Spirit not only imparts the conviction of the need of a Savior, but also imparts the faith to receive Him.

Never think it was *your* faith that received Christ as your Savior. Never say that any act of yours was the basis of your redemption. It is Jesus who imparts the water of which He spoke to the woman by Samaria's wayside well. It is Jesus who puts His arms of love beneath the burden on your back and lifts it from your tired, weary body. It is Jesus who pours into the lacerated, broken heart the oil of heaven's joy. It is Jesus who smoothes the wrinkles of care with the gentle touch of a mother's hand, and it is Jesus who brings you out of the darkness of the night into the light of His own glorious and wonderful day.

"Oh, it is Jesus; yes, it is Jesus;
Yes, it is Jesus in my soul;
For I have touched the hem of His garment,
And His blood has made me whole!"

Sing it and shout it. Proclaim it and herald it near and far. His blood—His grace—His power—His pardon—His *faith!*

A LIVING FAITH

When will we stop our foolish and needless struggles and begin to believe? When will we put an end to our unscriptural mental and intellectual gyrations in our attempt to find a faith we do not possess; for unless we get it from God, never will we possess that Faith! We are capable of belief and at the same time absolutely incapable of the exercise of Bible faith. Thousands have wandered into the error of thinking that belief is faith. *It is not.* There is belief in faith, without a doubt; but *"the devils also believe."* Belief is cold—intellectual. It operates as far as the human goes in the realms of intellect. Many sinful men believe the Bible, but such belief does not save them.

Faith is living. It moves and operates, and sweeps the enemies of the soul before its irresistible march. All the faith in the world? No! You need only as much as a grain of mustard seed, if it is God's faith! Then mountains will be removed. Your sin-sick soul will behold the glory of the Lord. But it must be God's faith. It must come from Him. He must impart it. And *He will.* That is the Gospel of grace that I believe.

The Jericho Road *without* Jesus is the Jericho Road. *With Him* it is the shining highway of salvation and healing. Its very rocks cry out His glory. *Without Him* its dust is sordid, its tears are real, and its blindness is so dark; but *with Him* its dust begins to grow the

> *When will we put an end to our unscriptural mental and intellectual gyrations in our attempt to find a faith we do not possess?*

flowers of grace and glory; its tears are turned to pearls; its blindness and darkness is turned to light. It takes the presence of Jesus to work the miracle of the transformation of the Jericho Road. The blind man did not sit in the sand and say to himself, "I am healed—I can see—I can see—now if only I can *believe* I am healed and can see, then I will be! No. He heard that Jesus of Nazareth was passing by. He cried, "Jesus! Jesus! Help me! Please help me, for I can not help myself!" Then do not forget the words of Jesus, "What wilt thou that I should do unto thee?" Mark you, it was not "What wilt thou that you should do," but "What do you want me to do?"

True, He said. "Go thy way; thy faith hath made thee whole." "Thy faith," said Jesus. Where did the blind man get it? Who gave it to him? If it was his faith all the time, why was he not healed before Jesus came that way? If you give me a watch, it is my watch. But I got it from you. There is faith in my heart as I write, but I know where I got it. Not affirmation—not from will—not from belief—not from mental grasps or understandings—but from Jesus. He is the Author and Finisher of *our* faith. Oh, matchless grace! Oh, love divine, all love excelling! Thus has the joy of heaven to earth come down!

Once upon a time there was a tiny little seed planted in the ground. It was an acorn. After a while it shed its little overcoat and cuddled away in the arms of Mother Nature, so that it might be fed and grow. All though the long winter night she kept that little seed warm; and when the springtime sun came out, its little acorn heart burst open with joy and delight. It started to grow. Then a man came along and put a big heavy rock over the little seed. It commenced to worry and to fret for fear it would never be able to raise its little head to where it could see the light of day. It wanted to wear a garland of leaves for its hair, and to grow to be beautiful and strong. One day its feeble hands touched the rock. They were such tiny, tender, little hands. The little growing tree felt so helpless. It did not struggle or try to move the rock that was the enemy of its heart and life. It just grew. One day the rock was lifted. It was pushed out of the way; and the little leafy hands clapped for joy. Who lifted the rock? The seed? No! It was something within the seed that no man in the world has ever been able to reproduce. It was God's power that pushed over that rock.

My friend, you are a little seed. You, too, can grow into something noble and beautiful for God. The power of faith can be manifested in your life until men and angels will wonder. However, when the battle is over and the victory has been won, do not say, "Look at what I have done through the Lord," but rather kneel at the foot of the cross and say, "Is it not wonderful that His grace and His faith should be manifested in me!"

5
Strength for Thy Labor

THE ONE OVERPOWERING impulse that has led me to write these words is the desire in my heart to show you the necessity of relying on and trusting in Jesus for all the needs of your life. How many times in life we see the tragedy of the collapse of the Christian who has to be brought low in order that he might once again recognize his true position in the grace of God. Self-righteousness is often born of continued victories. Because we overcome by God's power and are sustained by His grace, the feeling begins to develop in the heart that we have reached a position of impregnability; and pride starts to feed the spirit of self-righteousness. We become so sure of ourselves and our position that we are on dangerous ground indeed. "Let him that thinketh he standeth take heed lest he fall" (I Corinthians 10:12).

At the disposal of the consecrated child of God there has been placed the resources of that strength which God alone can provide. It is the recognition of the miracle of that vital contact, with its illimitable possibilities, that means victory over sin and self as we travel along the homeward trail. Lose that contact and you lose not only the hope, but also the possibility of a victorious life. You are dependent upon Jesus for everything. He gives freely. Whether or not you avail yourself of the opportunities, which His presence offers, is dependent entirely upon whether or not you have learned the secret of drawing on the master's strength.

Go back in the pages of the Sacred Word and get a glimpse of this stupendous revelation in God's dealings with Abraham the faithful. The first verse of the seventeenth of Genesis brings us into an understanding of the faithful purpose of the divine heart in a lesson so beautiful that men must stand in awe, and angels must wonder. The faith of Abraham was being tested. God had

made a promise. Never in all of time or eternity did He make one He was unable to fulfill! From the loins of the ancient patriarch was to come the seed through whose life and service all the nations of the world were to be blessed. Numberless as the stars of the firmament was to be his progeny. Upon that child was to be placed the hand of the Lord in benediction and in power.

Night after night the old man dreamed of the happy day when that promise would be fulfilled. But the sands in the hourglass on the mantel measured the passing of time. The lazy years drifted by and oh, how long and interminable they seemed. The boy did not come. Old Abraham was ninety, but still no fulfillment of the promise divine. Ninety- five, and still Sara and her husband waited in vain. Then came the year in which he looked forward to the turning of the century. He was ninety-nine; and yet there was no boy. Reason commenced to whisper things of fear in his ear. The ground began to tremble beneath the old man's feet. His faith began to slip. Up to this time his walk had been perfect—not in self—but in his Lord. He was getting miserable now. I presume more than once he had looked up at those same stars which he had seen on the night in which God had given him the promise; and the misty tears spread themselves like a film across his vision, until the stars seemed to dissolve in a sea of sorrow and disappointment. Reason said, "Abraham, this thing is impossible." He thought of Sara's age. He pondered over his own advanced years. How could this thing be? And yet—and yet—there was that promise! Long and fierce raged the battle in the old man's heart and mind. But there was the promise—from God Himself.

EL-SHADDAI

One night a voice spoke to Abraham's heart. He knew that voice. He lifted up his eyes in weakness and listened with his failing ears to the awesome intonation of the Voice which had spoken to him years before. Then God spoke, "I am the Almighty God; walk before me, and be thou perfect." What words! I am told that many Jews refuse to mention that majestic name of God, "El-Shaddai," but refer to that word as "The Name." What does it mean?

> *We believe that God gives it but we have not learned how to receive it.*

The word El means "God," or "The Strong One." Abraham might be weak, but God was strong. Men might be moved by the power of circumstance and the iniquitous forces of life, but God never. He is the Strong One. But what good does that do us? Suppose God is strong while we are so weak? To sit in our weakness, misery, and failure, and look at His strength only aggravates our lost condition. God is strong—no doubt about that—but what about our poor weakness and need? Then God spoke to Abraham. He said the glorious and wonderful words that like a rainbow of glory bridged the chasm between helpless man and omnipotent God. He said, "I am. El-Shaddai.

The word Shad is the Hebrew for "breast." It is used invariably throughout the Old Testament for the breast of a woman. It is the place from which baby lips derive the food that gives them strength. There is no sweeter picture on earth than that of a little child in its mother's arms. There is no symphony more beautiful than her baby's laugh. It is part of that mother's life; flesh of her flesh and bone of her bone. The life of the mother flows into the babe. Her strength, love, solicitude, and care all flow into the life and body of the sweet little bundle that is a part of her. Thus an eternal God wrapped up an infinite truth in the vocabulary of earth and gave it as a gift to Abraham and to you and to me.

What God meant was, "Draw from Me, Abraham. I am your strength. I am your sustenance. I am El, the Strong One, but I am also Shaddai, the Nourisher, and the Life-Giver. There is no need for you to falter, Abraham, no need to tremble and shake in your faith. Draw for your weakness from the fountain of my strength, even as a babe draws from his mother's breast the milk of life. No need to stumble over unbelief, Abraham, but *walk before me and be thou perfect,*" thus saith the Lord. That is the lesson. God is the source, the unfailing source, of the supply that is more than sufficient for all our need; of grace to cover all our sin; love that pardons all our iniquity, stripes that are sufficient for all our healing; strength for all our weakness. We believe that; but herein we have failed. We believe that God gives it, but we have not learned how to receive it. The mother gives the milk to her babe, but the little one must receive it. The infusion of the divine strength and nature is dependent upon two things: your knowledge that God is willing to give, and your learning how to receive. As unfailing as the law of the seedtime and the harvest; as irrevocable as the marching of the days and nights in their order is the great truth that God is always ready to meet your every need, if only you are ready to receive.

Praise His Name, He is still El-Shaddai! Does not Paul admonish us to become "partakers of the divine nature?" Has God Himself not told us, "My grace is sufficient for thee"? Back of all our vain glorying, our miserable spiritual pride and abhorrent self-righteousness is the God who loves us and gave Himself for us, and who longs for us to learn the lesson of drawing from Him all that we need for every moment of every passing day.

WHO?

Back yonder we see Elijah sitting in defeat and spiritual disgrace. He has quit. He of the lion heart has been beaten on the battlefield of the soul; and that after he bad faced an army! Then something happens. We watch him as he goes for forty days and nights without food, unto Horeb, the mount of God. In whose strength did he go? Who told David to advance in his natural weakness against the giant Goliath of Gath? Who guided the stone which sped unerringly on its way? Who gave his arm the strength, and his heart the courage? Who pushed down the walls of Jericho; and Who slew the host of Sennacherib when the Syrian came down like a wolf on the fold? Who delivered Israel, and Who led them in the exodus? Who opened the prison doors for Peter and Who pulled back the curtains of glory for Stephen, and gave him grace to pray for his murderers? Who dried the tears of Martha and poured oil into the broken heart of Mary? Who was it saved our guilty souls, when we knelt at the foot of the cross? Who turned our darkness into day? Who stands by our sides at this moment, ready and willing to give grace and glory? Who has strength for our weakness—healing for our sickness—power for our trials—freedom for our slavery—and grace sufficient for every need? Who can it be, but Jesus?

El-Shaddai still speaks to the hearts of men and, of a truth, we can still sing, "Strength for thy labor the Lord will provide." Reader, draw upon His Life. Take the grace He so freely and gladly imparts. He is more than sufficient for *your* need, and it is possible to walk before Him and be perfect, not in self, but in Christ. I know whereof I speak.

It has been my privilege to be called by my Lord to preach His gospel over the earth. The greatest joy of my life is to win souls, as He leads me and gives me strength for the task. Many of the campaigns run from eight to ten weeks, and sometimes the body gets very weary. One night I was sitting in an office in a corner of the tabernacle, feeling tired and at the end of my endurance. Out in the auditorium a great crowd was waiting for the service to begin, and through the thin boards I could hear the murmur of people at prayer. Then the door opened. A minister stood there and said, "Brother Price, there are about five hundred people here tonight who expect to be anointed in the name of the Lord for healing."

Five hundred—and I did not have the strength I needed to preach. Then there was that multitude to meet in the name of my Lord. In my heart I felt for a moment like running away. Then I wondered if I could dismiss the sick and tell them to come back some other night. I looked through a crack in the wall, and there I saw the poor sufferers waiting for a poor human like me to come and tell them of Jesus. Suddenly my nerves seemed to go to pieces. I dropped to my knees on the floor and wept. "Oh, Jesus," I cried, "I can't. I have not the strength. I am so weary and tired. I want to, Lord, but I am not equal to this task."

Then I heard that still small voice in the depths of my heart, "You have no strength; why not take mine?"

Then I heard that still, small voice in the depths of my heart. *"You have no strength. Why not take mine?"* For a moment I thought, *"could this be real?"* Why not? Did not the Lord give His strength to people in the olden days? Why not now? "Thank you, Lord," I said as I waited for what He would do. Then I felt a warm glow come over this body of mine. I walked out on the platform. Many times I preach from notes, but not that night. There was no weariness, no fatigue; nothing but the conscious knowledge of His strength. In faith I assured the sufferers that all would be reached that night. When the midnight hour came, I was still laying these unworthy hands of mine upon human heads, in the name of the Lord Jesus. The power of the Lord was present to heal them, because the Lord Himself was there. Then came the last one. I prayed; pronounced the benediction; and went home. As I was about to retire, I became conscious again of a great weariness. But I was not too tired to drop on my knees and thank Him for what He had done that night. He was still El-Shaddai. I knew that He had imparted *His strength* to meet my weakness. He will meet your weakness too. He will meet your every need, and no good thing will He withhold from them that walk uprightly.

One great requisite for the reception of the strength that He can give is that you feel your *need* of that strength. Our trust in Him is personal confidence; and when we come on the basis of His merit, He gives to us His faith. We do not look *at* Jesus, but *unto* Him. So many follow Him *afar off.* They look *at* Him; but are not near enough to look *unto* Him. They lag behind while they dissect creeds, handle dogmas, contend with others about interpretations, and lose thereby the sweetness of His presence.

Two men once came to me with a controversial question, and asked for my opinion regarding it. I listened to their statements; and when they had finished, I had to acknowledge that I did not know the answer. So I said, "Brethren, the important thing is not *what you* believe, but in *whom* you believe." You will perhaps at first be inclined to disagree with that statement on the ground that what you believe is of tremendous importance. Yet, when at last you reach the portals of "home," you will not tell the angels that you climbed to heaven on the rungs of the ladder of creed, but you will testify that you are at home because of the One who died for You on the Cross of Calvary.

WHICH WOULD YOU BE?

Have you then learned the lesson of drawing on Jesus for the needs of your life? Have you found the sweetness of abiding in the Lord? Have you come to

67

the realization that after all you are a miserable failure? Have you come to the place of the consciousness of your great need, and your pitiful lack of strength with which to overcome? Would you not rather be in the shoes of the Publican on the temple steps than in the shoes worn by the Pharisee who felt so strong in his righteousness and so proud of his deeds? Only as we *decrease* can Jesus *increase*. That means to decrease in our self-life, in our self-esteem, and in our self-confidence.

The house that was built on the sand felt proud of itself, until the wind began to blow and the tempest to rage. The house that was built on the rock cared not for the tempest, angry winds or waves; and when the lashing gales began to scourge it, it was able, having done all, to stand in the evil day. The strength was not in the house, but in the *rock*. It was not the house that gave the rock its strength, but it was the rock which gave strength to the house. Christ can be your all in all, not only in the picture that is framed in the border of a beautiful theology, but also in practice and reality every moment in every day of the passing years. He invites you to prove Him. He admonishes you to test Him. Why be empty when you can be full to overflowing? Why be hungry when you can be fed? Why wander like a lost child on the desert wastes of life, crying because you know not the way of your tomorrows? Better by far it is to put your hand in His and hear the whisper of His voice divine, "Follow me; I'll guide thee home."

Then the thing, undreamed of in any Arabian Nights of fiction, becomes real in Christ. The desert turns into a trail of flowers; and the heartthrobs pull at the bell ropes of heaven until the music of the skies is heard again by mortal ears. The rocky hills are but the paths which lead upward to a transfiguration trysting place, together with the saints; as we love Him, who leads and guides us, more and more with every step of the way. Oh, Soul of Mine, boast not now—nor in eternity—of your accomplishments in thought and deed. The star of feeble service seems dim indeed in the light which streams from the Cross. The labor of our human hands is forgotten as we look through our tears at the hands that were wounded on the Tree. The titles and degrees we bear in pride will hang their heads in shame, when they behold the inscription at the head of the Cross. The things we have done will seem so small in comparison with the things that He has done. How wonderful His leadership! How marvelous His grace! How far beyond the reach of the mind that has not been illumined by the power of the Holy Spirit is the truth that here and now He is willing to impart more than sufficient to meet our every need. He will do it now. He is still El-Shaddai, the God who is enough.

At a recent camp meeting an elderly lady listened to the truth set forth on this printed page. She was so very sick! Over and over again she had been anointed; over and over again to no avail. At the end of the service I saw her sitting quietly, but the expression on her face told me of the conflict within.

Suddenly she clasped her hands in prayer and said so appealingly, "Oh Jesus, I have tried so long with this poor faith of mine. Please give me some of yours." He did!

> *"Oh Jesus, I have tried so long with this poor faith of mine. Please give me some of yours."*

That is the secret of Christian victory. That is the secret of overcoming. Laying your burdens at His feet—to leave them there and never again carry them around like an old worn-out garment—is the confidence the Lord desires that we enjoy. That is the message of the God who is enough. Enough for whom? Why, for *you*, of course. Enough for when? For *now*, of course. That is the provision of El-Shaddai! Then as you march daily along the trail of time to the portals of eternity, you will be conscious of heaven on earth. As you draw nearer and nearer to the day when you can tell the angels you are coming, the songs of grace and glory will resound throughout the country of the homeward trail—His presence—His strength —His power—

His love—His faith—His grace—and
you will find yourself singing as onward
and upward you go,

"All the way my Savior leads me,
Cheers each winding path I tread,
Gives me grace for every trial, Feeds me
on the Living Bread.

"When my spirit cloth'd immortal Wings its
flight to realms of day,
This my song through endless ages, Jesus led
me all the way."

Oh, the wonders of El-Shaddai, the
God who is enough!

6
Your Mountains Are Moved

THE BETHANY ROAD twists and winds around the shoulders of the Hill, mounting in one direction higher and higher, until it comes almost abruptly to the walls of Jerusalem. In the other direction it coils downward toward the narrow defile and the rocky, inhospitable country that stretches away to the plains of Gilgal and the Dead Sea.

One day Jesus and His disciples were walking along that road on their way to Jerusalem. Jesus was hungry. That hardly seems possible, and yet He was. Imagine God being hungry in a world in which everything that grew was there because of His own creative genius and power. But Jesus was also human. When He left His throne and His kingly crown, it was to share with men the joys and sorrows and even the problems of everyday life. He not only knows all about our troubles, but He shares them with us, too.

On the hillside was a fig tree full of leaves. The Master and His disciples approached that tree to see if there were any figs thereon. It had nothing but leaves. No fruit hung on its branches. No figs presented themselves to the eyes. It was a fig tree without figs. So the Lord cursed it and declared that no man in the future would ever eat of its fruit, for never again would it bear any. Now why did Jesus do that? He knew there were no figs on it before ever He approached it. If He could see Nathaniel under the fig tree when he was out of sight, could He not see figs *in* the fig tree, if any had been there?

Jesus never did things without a purpose. There was a motive back of all His

> *Jesus not only knows about all our troubles, but He shares them with us, too.*

words and works. There must have been a meaning in the incident. There was a lesson He wanted to bring to the disciples *then*, for had the incident been devoid of teaching, it never would have happened. There was a lesson He wanted to preserve for you and me, for if there had been no such motive, would it ever have occupied such precious space within the covers of the Book? 'What was the lesson, and why was it taught?

Into Jerusalem went my Lord with His followers. Out of the temple they drove the merchandisers who were profaning the sacred place with their commercialism. The following day they were back on the Bethany Road. Peter saw the fig tree. He noticed it was dead—dried up—and withered. In amazement and surprise he cried out, "Master, behold!" and he pointed to the fig tree and called attention to the fact that it was withered away. Then Jesus spoke—not to Peter alone, but to *all* of them. Here was the purpose. Here was an object lesson that God, who became man, was going to use in order that men might understand God in their humanity. There *was* a motive behind the cursing of the tree. So Jesus said, "Have faith in God."

By my side is my Greek Testament. Let me quote word for word that entire sentence in the order in which the words come, remembering that the structure of Greek sentences is different from that of our English. Here is the sentence in the Greek: "And answering, the Jesus says to them: "Have you *faith of God?*" That is the actual, word-for-word translation from the original.

Then the Master went on to tell them that *if they had such a faith,* not only would a little fig tree dry up at the exercise of such faith, but that mountains could be removed and cast into the sea. The lesson was that of the irresistible power of the faith that was the faith *of God.* It was indeed mountain-moving faith. One of the requirements, as you will see by reading the record in Mark 11:22-26 is that there be no doubt in the heart

about the consummation of the miracle—nothing but a belief that the thing you desire and pray for *will* come to pass. When those conditions are met, then the miracle—whatever it is—has to happen; for back of it is the Word of God, and back of His Word is His power. It is His power which made the fig tree, the mountain, and everything that is; for it was the creative genius of the Eternal One, Who brought into being all things that are. His word brought cosmos out of chaos.

Now let us ask God to send the Holy Spirit with truth divine and bring the illuminating light of His presence to these minds and hearts of ours. Generally we interpret that scripture, "Have Faith in God," to mean that we have confidence in God's power to move a mountain. We say in our hearts, "If only I have faith enough *in* God; if only I can believe hard enough; and if only I can get doubt out of my heart, then God will move that mountain."

AN IMPOSSIBILITY

You are trying to do the impossible.

Your faith would never be strong enough or pure enough for that, though you were to struggle for a million years. What a mistake it is to take our *belief* in God and call it *faith*. How my heart has bled when I have seen some of God's dear children (and so have you) struggling to believe for victory over sickness, because they have not discerned the difference between belief in the power of God to heal (which belief even the devils have) and the *faith of God* which brings the victory. There is a great deal of difference between what we call the *faith of man in God,* and the *faith of God* that is imparted to man. Such faith is not the child of effort, neither is it born of struggle.

If it is the faith *of* God, then we get it *from* Him, and not from our mental attitudes or affirmations. Jesus did not say, "If you have the power to believe that God will remove that mountain, then He will do it." Neither did He say, "If you can believe hard enough that it

> *You simply cannot believe without the alloy of doubt until you have the faith of God.*

is done, then it will be done." But He did say, "*Have the faith of God.*" In other words, get some of God's faith; and then when you have that, you will have the only power with which mountains can be moved and cast into the sea. But you tell me that in the second part of His statement He talks about believing with the heart and having no doubts. The second is impossible without the first. You simply *cannot* believe without the alloy of doubt *until* you have the faith of God. It takes God's *faith* to clean up these human hearts of ours of all the debris, the fears, misgivings and doubts. The groans and the struggles we have heard come from people who have tried to believe it is done without having God's faith! They might have confidence in His power, and belief in His promise; but to possess His faith is something else.

All this has led me to believe that it is far more important that we seek the

Healer than healing. In the secret of His presence there is a hiding place for the soul. As the life empties itself of the world and its contacts, it makes room for the things that God can *impart*. Have you noticed that at the end of the statement our blessed Lord made to His disciples about the faith that would move mountains, He tells them to be sure to *forgive* everybody against whom they might have some grudge or feeling? Why does He say *that* in connection with this great lesson on mountain-moving faith? Is it not because of the fact that, when God would impart His faith to us, He does not want to find a channel that is choked by hate and an unforgiving spirit?

The frailties of human nature beset us on every hand and side; and the good Lord knows they do. With what patience and care He must watch over us and deal with us; and how many, many times His grace is wrapped around us like a blanket that covers our imperfections; and we hear His voice of love when we do not deserve it. Like as a father pitieth his children, so the Lord pitieth them that fear Him. I do not mean to imply that He demands perfection of life and conduct before He imparts the grace of His faith, but perhaps there will be things that He will require of us in order that His blessings He might impart. A God of infinite and eternal love wants no malice in the hearts of His children. How can we, who have been forgiven so much, refuse to forgive those who perchance have transgressed against us?

The meaning of the Lord is clear. He is saying that if we are to become the recipients of the faith that is the faith of God, then we must forgive all who trespass against us. It is into such a yielded heart—when the soul cries out its need of God because of its own helplessness—that the benediction of His faith comes; and with it the *consciousness* that it is there.

A WOMAN'S STORY

How well I remember a woman who came to the meetings some years ago in need of healing and prayer. She seemed to be such a noble character, and her family loved her devotedly and dearly.

One night we prayed for her in the name of the Lord Jesus, and she went away seemingly happy. She said she was standing on the promises of God; but she was not healed. As the days went by, two of her daughters came to see me, and begged me to pray again. As a matter of fact, they were almost hysterical in their anxiety and desperation. They loved their mother, and they knew that God was their only hope. They asked me to anoint her once again. I did!

Never shall I forget the pleadings, the importunities, and the frantic cries of those dear people as they stormed the throne of grace. They tried to believe; but it seemed to be all in vain. The poor, sick woman brushed the tears from her eyes as we sang, "Jesus breaks every fetter," and went away from the meeting without any evident answer to our prayer. Two days passed. Then she came early, before the service, to the office door. Here was a different woman! Her face was illumined by the glow of the glory in her soul. "You have been healed!" I said. She smiled, as she answered, "No, not yet; but I shall be

tonight. I have been prayed for publicly, and I believe my Lord wants to touch me by His power in the service tonight, so that all may see that He is faithful." There was no strained, tense atmosphere; no struggle; but rather, sweet and beautiful rest in the Lord. Then she told me her story.

Broken and crushed—almost in despair—she had gone home. She had come to the end of herself and she knew it. As she knelt by the side of her bed, and prayed, she sobbed: "Dear Jesus, I have *tried* so *hard* to have faith and I can't. I have failed, dear Lord, and yet I do believe in your promise and your Word. Brother Price has tried, and he has failed. The people in the meeting have tried, and they too have failed. Where can I go? What can I do? Speak to me, Lord. My only hope is in Thee." Then before her came the thought of a woman who had succeeded her as the teacher of a young people's class. Deep in her heart there had developed a feeling against that woman who had won the hearts of the young people, where once their love and affection had been showered upon her. Was it envy?

Was it jealousy? She knew not; but she did know that with the passing of the months the feeling had become intensified. Now she thought of her. She saw then the *true* condition of her heart. Perhaps she heard the Master say, "And when ye stand praying, forgive."

This very afternoon she had spent an hour in prayer with that woman, and God put in her heart a deep and beautiful Christian love for her. Sweet hour of prayer! Wonderful place of communion, where we talk to God, and in which God talks to us! The wounds are healed! The envy melted away, and the love of Jesus flowed in. When at last she arrived home, she told the family at the supper table that she would be healed that night. She knew it; but she did not know *how* she knew it. The consciousness of it was as real as life itself. There was no doubt about it. There was no intercession. That had been a work of the past. There was no agonizing and pleading. It was done; and yet it was not! That is the paradox of faith. Then she said to me, "My Brother, do you know what Jesus has done?" "I know that my Lord doeth all

things well," was my reply. "He has given me His faith," she said. "Honestly, I do not know the moment I received it; but, praise His name, I know it is here." And it was. That night the heavenly breezes blew. That night the Christ of the healing road touched, with the power of Omnipotence, the sick, weary body of His needy child. That night a cancer was melted by the touch divine. A mountain was moved by the *faith of God* that had been *imparted* to a sick woman by the Lord of Glory Himself.

SEEK THE HEALER, NOT HEALING

Our chief difficulty is that we seek healing instead of the Healer. Of what use is it to look for light and disdain the sun. The woman, recounted in the scriptures, who had the issue of blood was not struggling to grasp a lifeline of deliverance by the power of mental apprehension. All she wanted to do was to get to Jesus. All the poor, blind, miserable wretch on the Jericho Road did was to crowd into his heart-rending cry the story of his own helplessness, and his belief in the love, power, and compassion of Jesus of Nazareth. Even though our blessed Lord did tell him that it was his faith that had made him whole, yet I am sure that what faith he had was given him by the Lord Himself.

Can a man *generate* enough faith to find healing in walking a few feet on a dusty, Jericho road? The presence of the Nazarene was the *source* of faith in the days of old; and it is the *presence of Jesus* that is the *source of our faith* in these days of doubt and unbelief; even as Jesus said "Without me, ye can do nothing." Truly the disciples of Jesus love to read the twelfth chapter of Romans. It raises such wonderful possibilities in the standard of separated, consecrated, Christian living! It is the type of gospel, however, that carnal Christians do not like to contact. Paul is beseeching Christians—importuning

> *The presence of the Nazarene was the source of faith in days of old, and it is still the source of faith in thee days of doubt and unbelief.*

the children of the Lord—to go on from good to better and from there to better still. They are *not* to be *conformed* to this world; *but transformed—literally, transfigured.* It is to be brought about by the *renewing* of the mind. The Greek word is *renovation.* When you renovate a lawn, you rake out the old and put in the new. This renovation is necessary in Christian living before we can prove what is that good and acceptable and perfect will of God (Romans 12:2). When that has happened, what then should be our *attitude?* Paul continues in his writing, "For I say, through the grace *given* unto me, to every man that is among you, not to think of *himself* more highly than he ought to think, but to think soberly, according AS GOD HATH DEALT TO EVERY MAN the measure of faith." There is a declaration! God deals to *every* man his measure of faith. What measure? How much? That depends upon verses one and two. They come before verse three. The point is—God *gives the faith.* He measures it out! The Greek, in a word-for-word translation, says: "To each one has the God divided a measure of faith." Weymouth, in his translation in modern speech, says, "In accordance with the amount of faith which God has allotted to each one."

Do you not see how foolish we are to struggle, and to try to believe *mentally,* when we ought—according to the Word—to believe *spiritually?* There will be head belief, for the mind will acquiesce; but the *renewed* mind will say *Amen"* to all the works of grace, by faith. Fundamentally, faith is *born* in the heart. The heart will accept the *unreasonable.* It believes what mind says is impossible. It counts the things that are, as though they were not; and the things that are not, as though they were. *Faith puts strength* in Noah's arm to build for a hundred years, when there is no sign of flood. It *sends an army* marching around Jericho's walls, when reason says it would take a million years to wear out the foundations by the tramp of march-

ing feet. It *pulls a nation* to the edge of a deep and impenetrable sea, only to find that the gates of the "ocean" swing wide on the watery hinges of omnipotent power, and that the paths of men are laid in the depths of the sea. *It sends men,* without flinching, into furnaces of fire, *and preserves them* in the dens of lions. Faith *chases death away* from its vigil over bodies, *and it brings back the life* that had fled. Faith! *God's Faith!* Not weak, puny struggles to believe; *not* futile *efforts* to apprehend the powers of the Eternal. Can a teacup contain an ocean? Can a grain of sand envelop a planet? Can my poor understanding comprehend the glory of an omnipotent God? *Only* as His love divine is freely given, *only* as He chooses to reveal Himself to me, *can I understand* and then, *only in part,* for were we to behold the fullness of His glory, no flesh could survive in His presence. Only as He gives His pardon, am I saved. Only as He imparts His strength, can I fight the good fight of faith. Only as He gives His love, can I forgive my enemies. Only as He lifts me, can I rise above the world of sorrow and sin. Great is the Mystery of Godliness; and wonderful, beyond our dreams, is the

Plan of His Redemption!

Needy One, at the end of the Road of Self you will find Him waiting. The Author and the Finisher of your Faith is willing to meet you there. Back of you are the tears and the sorrows, the heartaches and the disappointments that are the gifts of a world devoid of faith and empty of belief in God; and the sunlit trail where Jesus stands, is bright and glorious with the light of His presence! Trust Him for His grace. Rest upon His promises. He is the Giver of every good and perfect gift; and the road up which you will walk, together with Him, will shine more and more unto the perfect day!

If you have *Salvation*, it will be because He has *imparted* it. If you have healing, it will be because of *His* virtue. If you have faith, it will be because *Faith has flowed out of His heart into yours;* and that is the *only* faith that can move your mountain. You can have it; for He will give it! Then will you know of a surety that the Faith—your *faith*, that has made you whole-is *a gift from God.*

7

God Wants to Make It Easy

I BELIEVE IT is easier to come to Christ, and to ask Him for the impartation of His Faith, than it is to *try* to work up and generate your own. Unless we look back of statements, which would be misleading were we to isolate them, we are in great danger of putting a wrong interpretation upon them. We must acknowledge that, in instance after instance, the Master mentioned the faith of the people who came unto Him; and on occasions He complimented them in His own beautiful way, because they possessed it. My question is not whether or not they had it, but *where did they get* it?

Samson had strength. With it he accomplished feats of power that were positively superhuman. But *where* did he get it? He was an example, in a physical way, of what we are admonished to be in a spiritual way. "Be strong in the Lord, and in the power of His might." Paul declared that he was strong; yet he continually acknowledged his weakness. But was he not the man who declared, "I can do *all things* through Christ which strengtheneth me"?

Do you remember that wonderful incident of the miraculous draught of fishes? The grey dawn of early morning was stealing over the blue waters of Galilee. The disciples had toiled *all* night, in their own strength, and had caught nothing. As they pulled in toward the shore, the Stranger of Galilee stood silhouetted against the green hillside, waiting for the coming of the men who were such *failures*. Then His voice rang out: "Children, have ye any meat?" They had none. They were returning from the toil of the long, weary night—absolutely empty-handed. He *knew* that. He knew that not even a minnow had been caught to give them so much as a light reward for the long, dark hours of labor and toil. Then He

told them to cast the net on the *other* side. As they obeyed, their eyes must have opened wide in amazement at the feel of the fish that were getting entangled in the net. They could not *pull* it in. In a minute they had caught more fish, following the instructions of Jesus, than they had caught in a *night* of their *own* endeavor. Wonderful story, you say? Yes, but I have not come to the most wonderful part of it yet! The most unbelievable and gloriously true part of the entire narrative comes in the next statement of Jesus. Talk about generosity! Talk about benevolence and graciousness! He said Bring of the fish which *ye have now caught."* Who caught those fish? Jesus said they did. But I ask you again, *Who caught those fish?"* You know, as well as I, who *caught* them. *It was Jesus.* Yet He said that they caught them. Thus He speaks of our faith and our love, of our this and that—as if we were anything at all—apart from *Him!*

HIS PERFECTIONS

Mark 5:27-28 gives us a beautiful illustration of this great truth. Alexander Maclaren says, "The main part of this story seems to be the illustration which it gives of the genuineness and power of an *imperfect* faith, and Christ's merciful way of responding to and strengthening such a faith." Look at the woman. She allows Jesus to pass. Then, timid and shrinking, she crowds her way to a place where she can touch His robe. Does she believe some peculiar kind of *magic* is connected with His cloak? After the contact had been made, she fain would have tried to *lose* herself in the crowd. The whole manner of her approach is evidence that she did not have what *we* have been in the habit of calling 'faith". She did not ask Him to speak a word! Yet, in her misery and ignorance, she approached the Lord and *touched* Him. She was healed! Instantly, too. The record states that virtue left the Christ, in order that the healing and the miracle might be consummated.

> *Healing is not dependent upon the development of a perfect faith by any processes of self, but rather contact with Jesus.*

The whole message of the story is the *fact* that such healing is not dependent upon the development of a perfect faith by any processes of self at all; but rather on that contact with Jesus, who is the Author and Finisher of our faith, and the giver of every good and perfect gift.

Let me again quote Dr. Maclaren:

"The power and vitality of faith is not measured by the comprehensiveness and clearness of belief. The richest soil may bear shrunken and barren ears; and on the arid sand with the thinnest layer of earth, gorgeous cacti may blossom out, and fleshy aloes lift their branches with stores of moisture to help them stand the heat. It is not for us to say what amount of ignorance is destructive to real confidence in Jesus Christ. But or ourselves, feeling how short a distance our sight travels and how little, after all, the great bulk of men in Christian lands know of theological truth, and how wide are the differences of opinion amongst us, and how soon we come to towering barriers beyond which our poor faculties can neither pass nor look, *it ought to be a joy to us that a faith which is clouded with ignorance may yet be a faith which Christ accepts.*"

That is my point. He supplies the deficiency. He makes up the need. When Jesus descended the mountainside from the scene of His transfiguration glory, He found a miserable, unhappy father and a group of impotent disciples trying to do by *their* faith what could be done only by the Faith of the Son of God. The man was honest when he said, *Lord I believe; help thou mine unbelief.*" Has not the scene of those disciples, struggling and shouting, rebuking and trying to cast out the devil—without success, been duplicated over and over again in modern days? But when Jesus walked on the scene, how quickly and beautifully the entire atmosphere was changed and transformed.

Out of the storm there came the calm.

Out of the tempest there was born a beautiful peace. Jesus was Master of the situation, and happy was the man who beheld that day the approach of a tender, sympathetic heart which was moved with compassion, and overflowing with divine love. The great essential is that we talk with Jesus; cease our struggle, and turn from our intercession to that trust and confidence in Him which will invite the impartation of the *faith* which He alone can give.

For twenty years and more I have been conducting campaigns in which a prominent place has been given to prayer for the sick and the suffering. To this ministry my Lord has called me, and to that call I have responded with all my heart. To His glory and praise, I record that I have seen the eyes of the blind opened. Miracles of power divine have raised cripples and paralytics from their wheel chairs and cots, and cancers and tumors have melted by the healing power of our wonderful Lord. But do you know what I have noticed? All *great* healing services have been preceded by nights of consecration and seasons of prayer. When the crowds have rushed forward, seeking *healing*, the meetings have been hard and difficult. When they have sought the *Healer*, rather than the *healing*, however, the sweetness of His presence has broken the *power* of the enemy; and the *sunshine* of His presence has melted the icy feeling that gripped the heart. It may be self-pity, or even self-love, which brings us to His feet; but our whole viewpoint is changed—once we are there—as *we at last see Him!*

THE POOR AND THE RICH

It is the poor and the needy who have been given so many good things, and it is the rich whom he has sent empty away. A crippled man was brought to the meetings some years ago. Those who brought him told me he was a man possessed of all the faith in the world and one who was known in the community for his good life and works. He was a good-living man and, no doubt, loved his Lord; but he was to go away from more than one service because of the *one thing* that he lacked, and which His Master was ultimately to reveal to his mind.

How the people prayed for that cripple! I can see him now, struggling to rise in answer to the entreaties of the people that he arise in faith and walk. Many times I knelt by the side of his chair and rebuked the power that bound him. The days went by and yet there was no sign of his healing—no acquiescence had come from the skies in response to prayer. One afternoon they wheeled him to a corner in the building. He asked the people to leave the two of us alone, and then said something that has lingered in the chambers of my memory. "What a failure I am," he declared. " I came here strong in what I thought was *my* faith in the Lord. As I look deeply into my heart I find something about which I wish to confess. What a poor, miserable failure I have been. I have been spiritually proud of the fact that people have pointed to *me* as a man who suffered without complaining. They pointed me out as the man who never grumbled, although he had a cross to bear. I grew proud of my reputation and I can see now that what I termed my goodness has been self-righteousness in the sight of my Lord."

He put his face in his hands and wept. There was something so pathetic about that poor, crippled man that the tears welled up in my eyes too. I reached out my hands and put them on his head and commenced to pray. I prayed for his healing; and, as I prayed, he stopped me. "Dr. Price," he said, "I don't need healing half as much as I need Jesus. I am so hungry for His presence. More than anything else in my life, I want to know Him better, and I am content to spend my days in this chair if only He will flood this self-righteous heart of mine with His peace and love." So I watched the cripple in the wheel chair disappear around the corner of the building. He went away quietly, and my heart went with him, as they wheeled him out of the building. All the way home my heart was singing for him the hymn:

Savior, Savior, hear my humble cry;

> *"I don't need healing half as much as I need Jesus. I am so hungry for His presence."*

While on others Thou art calling,
Do not pass me by!

A broken and a contrite heart will He not despise! How sweet it is to come to the end of self! How wonderful, after we have toiled all night and have caught nothing, that He condescends to wait for us on the shore! How gracious the voice that tells us to cast our nets on the *right* side of the boat, that our joy might be full! What determines which is the right side of a boat? Why, the way it is going, of course. You will soon find out where the right side is *if your boat is going toward Jesus;* and the boat must be *empty,* if you would *bring* the Nazarene on board.

A few days later I was leaving the building in company with Dr. Manchester, the man who buried President McKinley. At the door of the auditorium sat the man in his wheel chair, patiently waiting for the doors to open for the evening service. The afternoon meeting was over. Dr. Manchester looked at the face of the crippled man and stopped. Then he walked over to him and I followed. "Are you coming for prayer?" he asked. "For prayer and to receive healing," was the reply. There was something different about the man. His voice —his tone—his eyes—such a look of reflected glory on his face. I knew something had happened. "Tell me," I said, "What has happened? My brother, I discern you have experienced something that is so wonderful I can feel its glory, though I do not know what it is."

Then he told me he had been with Jesus. He had spent the night in prayer—not in intercession alone, but in praise and worship. He told me that at four in the morning a consciousness of the presence of his Lord had overwhelmed him. He knew Jesus was in his room in a special way. He told me how his voice in adoration had commenced to praise his Lord. He said that he then became conscious of an infusion of the Life Divine. Something passed from Jesus to him; and he felt as though a fog

had rolled away from his heart and mind. From that moment on he knew his struggles were over; and a sweet and holy peace was wrapped around his soul. He told us that now he *knew*, when once again he came to obey his Lord in the anointing with oil, strength would flow from Jesus, and life divine would be given him to restore him to health and strength.

As I looked into Dr. Manchester's face, I noticed that tears stood in his eyes. Then he spoke, "Why does this man have to wait until tonight?" "He does not," I replied. "The Great Physician is here now. Jesus of Nazareth is passing by." A moment later it was over. Out of his wheel chair arose that man. He ran and jumped and praised the Lord for his deliverance. It was a miracle of power divine. Around him on the snowy street, men and women gathered first to praise, and then to pray. Unsaved hearts were broken, and many were the penitential tears that were shed!

More than once I have been with a group of disciples, struggling at the foot of a mountain; and oh, how my heart can testify to the difference it makes when into the midst of our helplessness Jesus Himself comes walking!

YOUR PRAYERS ANSWERED

Do you not know that your prayers can be answered? Do you not know that *your* burdens and cares can be left at His feet; that you never need bow your shoulders again with the weight of sorrow and care? I am praying, please God, that thousands who will read these lines will come to the place of abandonment of the trail of self-endeavor, realizing that it has led them into doubts and fears which destroy confidence and trust in God. Know ye not that faith cometh by hearing, and hearing by the Word of God? In my Greek Testament it reads, "and hearing *by a word of God.*" There is a finer ear than the one with which we listen to the music of the organ in the church service. There is another ear than the one we use when we listen to the reading of the grand old Book. It is not merely the intonation of a human voice that speaks as the Bible is read, for men hear that Book and yet do not hear the voice of God. The Bible is a book through which God speaks; yet all do not hear His voice in the lines! Faith cometh by hearing, and hearing by a *word* of God. Let Jesus speak to this heart of mine and doubts will take the wings of the morning and fly away. Let Jesus breathe a little word to this poor mind of mine and heaven is brought to earth Fear is gone like a shadow in the light of His glorious truth. Let Him say, "Bring him to me," and then cometh faith—God's faith—His faith—and my poor heart will cry, "Lord, that I may receive my sight." Let Jesus breathe on me, with His love and presence, and mountains will commence to tremble, and the fingers of the foundations will

> *The Bible is a book through which God speaks; yet all do not hear His voice in the lines! Faith cometh by hearing.*

lose their grip!

That is how faith comes! Not through the channels of human concepts. Not along the paths of human understandings. Not by the abilities of minds to comprehend, or the power of the intellect to affirm. Reach with fingers such as those for the moon and you will struggle and groan in vain to possess it. But let Jesus speak, and the soul is lifted. One little word from Jesus is worth all the words in a dictionary of human language.

There is hope for the blind Bartimaeus of the Jericho Road of today, when Jesus of Nazareth is passing this way. "Hope," did I say? Yes, hope-and more than hope; for when He hears our cry of helplessness, He will not pass us by. . .When He speaks, hope is kindled until it becomes a fire that burns away all doubt and unbelief, and the warmth of a divine and beautiful faith brings healing to the soul.

[handwritten marginal note: sometimes it is incrementally - all we are capable of, day by day re affirmed, strengthened, becoming more certain & sure]

O Master, speak! In our need and self-helplessness, we would lift our hearts and voices to Thee. Speak the word—

that will be all we need. We have tried, with the broken cisterns of our faith and endeavors, to believe; but their waters have failed!

Savior, Savior, hear my humble cry;
While on others Thou are calling,
Do not pass me by!

8
Imparted Faith

THE BELLS OF my heart are ringing, because I know that my Lord is able to supply all our need. The storehouses of grace are filled to overflowing and the quantity is of such abundance, that it is inconceivable to these hearts and minds of ours. We deal with earthly and temporal limits, while God deals with the illimitable and eternal. The measure of God's giving is always to overflowing. The apostle stated, "Who giveth to all men liberally"; and there is no end to His beneficence, and no lack in His inexhaustible supply.

Does it not seem tragic that, with all this, there is such spiritual poverty? Is it not a matter that should cause us to pray, and to seek His face, in order that we may discover the link that is missing in the chain of revealed and recognized truth? Surely when He has *enough*, and that enough is *backed* by His *promise*, then undoubtedly there is something missing *somewhere* when we continue in our sorrows and our needs. In this Dispensation of Grace, with an open door to the presence of God Himself, we can arrive at but one conclusion: *that faith is the quality or power by which the things desired become the things possessed.* It is the substance of things hoped for, the evidence of things not seen. That is the nearest to a definition of what faith is— even in the Inspired 'Word. In spite of its potency, it is somewhat of an intangible commodity. You can't weigh it, or confine it in a container. It is almost like trying to define energy, in the realm of physics, in one comprehensive statement.

We are told that the atom is a world within itself, and that the potential energy contained within such a tiny "universe" is so great that it makes the mind of the layman bewildered. But define it—or attempt to—and you will run into difficulties. Faith too is like that. There have been times when I have felt it stealing over the soul, until I have dared to say and do things which, had I allowed reason to take charge of affairs, I would have hesitated to say and do. Though it came, perhaps, only as big as a grain of mustard seed, it flowed though word and act with irresistible power, until people stood in wonder at the mighty works of the Lord.

> *Neither in me nor in you are the ingredients or qualities to make even a mustard seed of Bible faith.*

One thing I *do* know, and that is, I cannot produce faith. Neither in me—nor in you—are there the ingredients or qualities which when mixed, or put together, will make even a mustard seed of Bible faith. If this be true, are we not foolish to attempt to bring about results without it? If I want to cross a lake, and find there is no way to reach the other side, except by boat; would it not be foolish of me to struggle to get across without a boat? The thing I should seek is the boat—not the other side of the lake! Get the boat, and it will take you there.

There are certain things that we receive by faith and only by faith. There is not the slightest ambiguity regarding that in the Word. Rather it sets forth a clear declaration of the truth. Now where do we get the faith that will take us across our "lakes"? The answer to this question is positive and sure! Between the covers of the sacred Book there is mention made of faith as the *gift* of God and faith as a *fruit* of the Spirit. 'Whether it be gift or fruit, however, the source and origin of faith remains the same! It comes from God There is no other source of faith; for it is the "Faith *of* God!

Suppose you could obtain faith by mixing any spiritual qualities, you might like to mention, in the crucibles of life. Suppose that faith was something *you* possessed. Now we all know of its power! Would it not be a *dangerous* possession? Suppose we could *use* it to cross the lake" when God wanted us on this side? Suppose you or I had faith

enough this morning to raise up every sufferer among us. If we were to utilize such power, how do we know but what we might be contravening the divine will, and overthrowing the divine plan?

A HIDDEN DANGER

Some time ago a lady brought to me a little girl who was sick. She was a sweet little tot, pretty as a picture, quiet and retiring; but a serious malady had fastened itself upon her little body. The father of the little girl, though he loved her dearly, was rebellious against the Lord. For years his wife had prayed for him to surrender, but he had always offered some excuse. We prayed together. Three times that little one was brought for prayer. Had there been *faith,* she would have been healed. But she was not! The mother went to prayer! Later she called me on the telephone and said, "Dr. Price, I feel that God is dealing with my husband. He loves our little girl so much that I think the Lord can reach his heart through her. Would it not be wonderful if I could get him to come with us when you pray once again? Perhaps, if we could get him on his knees to pray for her, it would not be long before he would be praying for himself."

The next time they came to the house for prayer, he came along. He was courteous, kind, and solicitous about his little girl; but when I asked him to pray, he said, "No, I don't want to be a hypocrite." The Holy Spirit led me to admonish him: "Brother, get on your knees, and let us look to the Lord together. If you do, I believe you will take a little girl home who has been healed by the touch of the Savior's hand." He looked at me in amazement, and said, "Do you really believe that?" I told him I did. Down on his knees went that man! There sweetly stole over the body of the little girl the healing virtue of Jesus; and she raised her expressive eyes to God in a prayer of thanksgiving and gratitude. 'While the father was searching and yielding his heart, the Savior spoke to him those words which to an unregenerate heart bring peace. Suppose I had possessed faith enough and could have used it at will. Would that have brought as much glory to the name of the Lord—to say nothing of the knowledge of sin forgiven to a heart-hungry father—as the *imparted* faith which was given at the time it was needed?

Many years ago, while I was in a Vancouver, B. C. Campaign, an incident occurred which kept me awake most of the night, with my heart open before the Lord. I had been praying for hundreds that night. There was in that meeting the very real consciousness of the sweet and wonderful presence of the Savior. Many weary, tired bodies had been renewed by the touch of the Master's hand. They had found deliverance from their pains and sicknesses, as they knelt at the foot of the cross. I turned to Dr. Gabriel Maguire, pastor of the First Baptist Church, and said, "The Lord is imparting faith tonight; the power of the Lord is present to heal." He replied that he was never more conscious of the moving power of God in all his life.

A minute later, together we placed our hands on the head of a man. A feeling akin to a vacuum came over me. I felt so *empty*. The presence of the Lord was with me, but I had no confidence or faith to pray for the man, and nothing happened to him! I prayed again. Then I felt so empty that I was about to cry out to the Lord and ask why He *seemed* to have departed when He had been so sweetly manifest just before. Instead, I turned to the man and said, "Brother, *why* are you here? Who are you? What is the *purpose* of your coming to the platform?" He turned pale. Then he made a confession! He told me that he was a professional *hypnotist*. He had stated that the power in the meeting was the power of hypnotism. He had argued with other people about it, and then had decided to use himself as a test case; as he wanted to investigate first-hand. Then, he planned to hold a public meeting and expose the whole divine healing movement. Now *this* man had a sickness, indeed! He *needed* healing; but suppose I had possessed faith for him. Would it not have been disastrous to have brought healing to that man? For, remember, if faith is powerless—it ceases to be faith.

You can't have faith without results any more than you can have motion without movement.

The thing we sometimes call "faith" is simply *trust*. We trust in the Lord; but faith has feet and wings and power. A man could not have *faith* for salvation and not be saved. He could *trust* the Lord, and promise that some day he would come to Christ, but when he has *faith* for salvation, it means he *is* saved.

> *The thing we sometimes call "faith" is simply trust.*

So it was with the man whose case I have just recounted. Whatever faith was given during the evening was withdrawn from me until I was praying for someone, who in the providence and will of God, was ready to receive from Him the blessing He alone can impart. It so happened that the very next one for whom we prayed, a woman, was one of the *outstanding* miracles of the entire campaign.

No Christian is entirely devoid of faith. It is implanted in the heart as a gift, or a fruit—faith enough to maintain your salvation; faith enough to obey the Lord, and do the things that are pleasing in His sight; but you are continually dependent upon Him for its perpetuity. You cannot keep the light and dismiss the sun. You cannot have faith in God, unless you have the *faith of* God. That is why the Scripture says, "By *grace* are ye saved, through *faith;* and that not of yourselves; it is the gift of God."

Grace and faith are so closely related that you cannot separate them. The wonder of it lies in the fact that faith is many times imparted when we feel the least deserving. It is not always the product of merit. Is not that gift of *faith* the beautiful flower of grace? That faith, which quiets the restless sea of life, makes *happy* the heart in the knowledge that the Pilot will see us *through*. Has that priceless possession come because of what we have given or done?

That faith—given me to touch the hem of His garment and be lifted above and out of my pain and suffering—dare I for a moment say that I received it because of my deeds and words? The faith which was yours in the hour of your trial—the opening heaven in vision beside the open grave—the angel music sounding through the heart when grief was moaning, and the poor heart aching and nearly breaking—how did it come, and why? When I survey the wondrous cross, I begin in part to understand why grace smiles on faith as it goes on every mission and ministry of life.

WHAT MANNER OF MAN

The disciples and the Master are on the waters of Galilee. The lake, which was so calm, is lashed into fury by the coming of the storm. The same lake, the same waters, and—perchance—the same day! The affrighted disciples are terror-stricken at the raging of the tempest and the fury of the winds, even as you and I would be. How quickly the scenes of life can change! It does not take long for laughter to be drowned in tears and a happy heart wrung by the cruel grip of sorrow. The incident of the storm and the calm did not happen merely for *them;* it happened because God wanted to speak also through it to your heart and mine.

When at last the disciples awakened the sleeping Christ, He asked them a question. You remember it well! It was, "*Where is your faith?*" Where was it? Had it dropped into the depths of the sea on which they sailed? Had it fled on the shoulders of the storm? Had it been dissolved in the spray that washed their boat? Their faith was with them all the time. The mistake they made was in forgetting the *fact* of *His* presence, while discerning the *fact* of the storm! Their faith was not far away. Remember the words of our Lord, "Without me ye can do nothing."

Then Jesus advanced to the bow of the boat. He looked into the face of the tempest and hurled His command into the teeth of the storm. The waves obeyed. The wind halted in its tracks. Jesus had spoken, and the disciples stood awed in the presence of His power. Where was their faith? Do you not know? Can you not see? It was just as near to them as it is to you and me; for let me assure you that the fact of the storm does not mean that He has gone! To be needy is no proof that you have been deserted. It may be the door that leads to a miracle! It may be God's method of making you say, "What manner of man is this, that even the wind and the seas obey Him?"

Can you imagine Peter, standing in that boat, telling those waves to be still? I can—if the Master of the sea had imparted faith for the miracle, and that in accordance with His will. It was Peter who confidently ministered in sublime spiritual bravery to the man at the beautiful gate. The man was healed, and he followed Peter and John into the Temple, shouting the praises of God as he went. "Such as I have, give I unto thee," said Peter, and he proved that he had it. But where did he get it? He had just come from an upper room and that upper room had contained the secret that was back of the healing by the Beautiful Gate. So conscious was Peter of the fact of the *Divine Impartation*, that he spent the greater part of his sermon, that followed the healing, telling how weak he was and how strong His Savior was. It was not *they;* it was not *their* power; it was their *Lord*.

How different this truth is from our

poor feeble attempts to transfer faith from the heart to the mind; to turn faith from a grace-imparted to a cold, intellectual assent or belief; to look for it in the unholy corridors of the will, rather than in the light which streams from heaven through the windows of the soul. There is a great deal of difference between the cripple who struggles and tries to walk and the cripple who looks and prays for the faith by which he will walk; and in my own heart I know that such faith is given while the soul waits before God, in the quiet and beautiful attitude of trust and rest in His promises, rather than in the turbulent atmosphere of our noisy strivings and endeavors. "Wait, I say, on the Lord. Rest in the Lord! Wait patiently for Him and He shall bring it to pass."

Roll on, blue waves of Galilee! Blow and moan, ye winds that rage, and ye tempests that blow. You laugh at my seeming helplessness. You ridicule my endeavors to stand in the midst of the rocking of the boat. You ask me where my faith is. You taunt me about my condition. My Faith is not far away! He sleeps awhile, to teach me to rely upon Him. He sleeps, that confidence in self might be turned to trust in His promise and in the power of His presence. No, my Faith is not far away. I look at Him and smile; for His voice whispers to this poor heart of mine, and tells me that if He can rest in the midst of the tempest and the storm, then I can sweetly rest in Him.

9
Faith is a Gift

FAITH IS ONE of two things. It is either a gift of God, or a fruit of the Spirit. Of that there cannot be the slightest doubt. Search the corridors of reason, and you will inevitably arrive at the same answer. If it is true that faith "as a grain of mustard seed" contains the dynamics which would move mountains, do you think God would entrust to our possession a weapon as potent as that? To have it otherwise, than as God has ordained, would not only destroy the entire economy and system whereby the Christian can walk in harmony and communion with God, but would put in the hands of weak people, such as you and I, an instrument which could be used for our destruction.

I do not mean that we would use faith

for physical manifestations alone; but that the spiritual reactions would prove to be a curse instead of a blessing, and impediments to growth rather than help. More than once I have tried to exercise faith, and have struggled to obtain the answer I desired to my prayer; only to find, in the light of succeeding events, that it was better by far that the prayer was not answered as I had desired.

That is why God deals to every man the measure of faith he needs to walk in harmony with the Divine Will. Beyond that point, faith will not be imparted. This lesson to me is so beautiful that it awakens in my heart a song of thanksgiving and praise to the Lord I love and serve. Perhaps I do not understand the purposes of God, but trust holds on when faith is not imparted: and I am happy in the consciousness that He is working in my life for the very best.

We should trust Him when we cannot see, and rely upon Him when we cannot understand. However, let us not make the mistake of calling that trust faith. Faith works, moves, operates and accomplishes things according to its measure and its power. Of course, to each one there is given the faith by which we call ourselves the children of God; and there is given or imparted to us the faith by which we daily know that we have passed from death unto life.

Faith is measured in the scales of God, even as we measure the commodities of earth. More than once our blessed Lord talked about little faith and great faith. He mentioned weak faith and strong faith. As we need the gift or fruit of faith, it is imparted by the Lord, in order that *God's will, rather than ours,* will be done on earth, and in us, even as it is in Heaven. There are many times when *our desires* are contrary to the will of God. Many times in our ignorance we would do the thing which would bring sorrow instead of joy. If we possessed the faith, for use at any and all times to bring about our own desires, it is clearly to be seen that the results would be disastrous.

The Christian world looks to the life of George Muller as a latter day example of the power of faith in the heart of a man who believed God. Such a life it was—a magnificent array of miraculous answers to prayer. In reading after his biographers, however, have you not noticed the fact that he *knew* he was in the center of God's will? There were hungry little mouths to be fed and little orphan bodies to be clothed; and Muller believed that the Lord, who called him to that ministry, would supply every need. So when the need arose, faith was given.

There was no struggle, no agonizing, no battle against doubt; only the manifestation of an *imparted* faith.

FAITH IS A GIFT

He was an ardent believer in fervent, effectual prayer. Many times he reveals the depth of his ministry of intercession. The reason, he says, that so many people fail to have their prayers answered is that they have not learned the value of importunity and continuity in prayer. Yet, whenever he came up to a crisis, he would tell the Lord his need in a most matter-of-fact way, and simply count it done by *faith*. If we are to

believe his writings, it was almost as simple as a woman stepping to her telephone, calling up the grocery store, and asking for the delivery of her needs. Thus Muller prayed to God!

Can you have faith like that in *yourself?* Can you possess such ability, apart from the gift and anointing of the Spirit of God? To endeavor to exercise something we do not possess leads to excesses in the realm of the spiritual; and often the attempt to use faith we do not possess drives out what little *trust* we have in God. Let me illustrate what I mean by the *impartation* of faith.

THE MASTER KNEW

Some years ago I was conducting a meeting in a Presbyterian Church in Medford, Oregon. The Lord led us to hold a healing service one afternoon. The place was crowded, and many were standing outside and on the window ledges, looking into the building. One of that number was a little crippled boy who walked with the aid of crutches. My heart bled for the little fellow, for there was such a look of pathos about his blue eyes that my heart was stirred. Silently I lifted my heart to the Lord, and asked for faith for the healing of the little lad.

Then across the platform there came for prayer a line of children, most of whom were accompanied by their parents. A little girl stood in front of me. Her mother was weeping. I laid my hands on her head and prayed. Nothing happened; but the spirit of the meeting seemed to change. There was a deadness and a heaviness which weighed heavily upon me. I prayed again; and the feeling seemed to increase. I looked at the weeping mother in bewilderment. She was sobbing. At last she cried out, almost hysterically, "Why won't Jesus heal my girl?" "Where do you worship?" I asked. "I go to the Methodist Church," was her reply.

> *As we need the gift or fruit of faith, it is imparted by the Lord in order that God's will—rather than ours—will be done.*

I looked at her closely. Then into my heart there came a suspicion. Just at that moment the Lord imparted the gift of discernment to one of the people by my side who asked the woman this question: "Have you ever been in Mysticism or Occultism?" She had, she confessed. Her little girl did *not* go to the Methodist Church. She, herself, had not been there for months. She had been attending a spiritualist séance week after week. Then I knew why my Lord had withheld His blessing and His faith. The mother continued to cry in her agony of soul, "He has healed others; please ask Him to heal my little girl." I said, "Sister, do you know anything about salvation through the shed blood of Jesus on Calvary?" She said she had at one time, but a sorrow had come into her life and, instead of taking a little tighter grip on the hand divine, she had turned away from God. In response to

102

my appeal, she said that she would like to give her heart to Christ then and there, and asked me to pray for her. She repeated a prayer of surrender after me, and then I closed with the words, "I am trusting in Jesus as my personal Savior, and I claim the promise of the blood as the atonement for all my sin."

Into my heart—and into hers too there swept a glory wave from heaven. As I reached out my hand once again to her little girl, I knew that her days as a cripple were over. She sprang to her feet. She was healed! Then I looked at the poor little crippled boy and held out my hand for him to try to climb through the window and come to the platform for prayer. He did not *come*. Instead, he fell through the window, leaving his crutches on the outside! He too was healed.

The Holy Ghost took such charge of that service, that I have seldom seen anything to equal it. Not only were people healed, but many were saved. Down the aisle came a dear, old lady who had been in a wheel chair for years. She was leaping, shouting, and praising God, even as they did in the days when the Savior walked the streets with men.

What a meeting! What a time to make men adore Him and angels to rejoice. Now, *suppose I had possessed faith for the healing* of that little girl. Suppose that when I first laid hands on her head, she had gone away well. Her mother would have taken it as a sign that the séance was in the order of the Lord, and from that moment on she would have been more deeply enmeshed in the Spiritism that I do not believe is of God. So, when I prayed in my lack of understanding, the spirit of faith and assurance was lifted from me. How empty I felt. Then, when the mother accepted Jesus as her personal Savior, faith was *imparted* and the work was done. Instead of struggling to be healed, how much sweeter and richer life would be, were we to look to Jesus who is "the Author and the Finisher of *our* faith."

A HAPPY MORNING

One March morning, some years ago, I left home feeling the love and presence of the Nazarene in my heart. I was on my way to pray for a poor woman who had lost her mind, and who was confined in an institution set apart for such sufferers. I can hear now the sobs of her husband, as he cried in desperation from the broken condition of his heart. Disaster—suddenly, without any warning—had struck a beautiful home with the rapidity of a lightning flash.

God was their only hope, and they knew it. I was anxious to pray for that woman and had gone forth confident that the Lord would hear and answer prayer. She was in such a helpless condition, and in the grip of an evil spirit! When at last I arrived at her room, she cried out in blasphemy and obscenity in a voice that was not her own.

That morning we saw no visible answer to our prayers; but the poor, distracted man grasped me by the lapels of my coat and hoarsely insisted that we refuse to give up and instead keep storming the Throne of Grace for the healing which Jesus alone could give. Accordingly, I called my church to prayer; and called other churches too. We agreed to pray for an entire day for the deliverance of the poor sufferer, and more than one prayer warrior resolved to stay upon his knees until the woman was delivered.

About four o'clock that afternoon, while praying near the altar of the church, I felt the Spirit of the Lord come upon me. Under the impulse of that anointing, I stood to my feet, and trembling with emotion and the glory of His presence, I announced that our prayers had reached through, and that the answer we desired was on the way. I stepped to the telephone and told the husband of the woman, that I believed we had received the victory. We had!

The following day, after a brief season of prayer and anointing, she arose in victory and triumph, and went home once again to her adoring husband and children. I knew the moment the evil spirit left her body. I was conscious of the moment he released his grip upon her poor soul.

I knew that the Faith of the Lord Jesus Christ had been given—released—at that moment of victory. I could not release His Faith myself; if I could have, in my limited understanding of God's purpose, she would have been healed the first time I prayed. But it was not until the Lord, in His Omniscience, released in me the faith he had imparted in love and grace, that the miracle of healing took place. Our possession of The Faith, as a grain of mustard seed, is ever subject not only to His *impartation* but also to *His control.*

A woman said to me the other day, "Pray for me, please. I have all the faith in the world." I knew what she meant. We hear that expression so many, many times. My reply was, "Sister, if you have that much faith, *why are you sick?"* She looked at me strangely. Then, after a few moments of thought, she went away to pray for faith, "as a grain of mustard seed."

> *Our possession of the faith as a grain of mustard seed, is ever subject not only to His impartation but also to His control.*

I am standing now in spirit, even as I write, on the hills of retrospection. I am looking back over the way my Savior has led me. I can see the campaigns, in Canada and the United States, in which by the grace of God I have been privileged to pray for as many as ten thousand people in a single month. One cannot do that without having some experiences stamped indelibly on the mind. In one meeting the atmosphere will be tense and hard; prayer seems to be in vain, and our efforts to bring victory meet with seeming failure. Then a sweep of glory and a rush of the power of the Holy Spirit will lift an entire audience to the portals of Heaven. There I have felt the kiss of the breezes of Heaven on my cheek, and have seen audiences so transported and lifted in spirit that they have sung with truth, "This is like heaven to me." Such meetings have only emphasized the great truth that man *in himself is* helpless before "the powers of the air" and that there must be a manifestation and evidence of the presence and power of the Lord Himself.

"Without me," said the Savior, *"you can do nothing."* We reply foolishly sometimes, "Oh, yes, I can, for *I have the faith.* I can use it, exercise it, and bring things to pass with it, for the Word says that if we have faith, we can move mountains." To such, I would say, "GO ahead, try it, and see what is the result."

All things are possible to them that believe. But it is important *what* you believe. To believe that you, apart from grace and divine impartation, are the possessor of a power that can move mountains is dangerous indeed. I know many who have tried such a program in their own strength, and perchance on the basis of self-righteousness, but sorrow has been their lot, instead of joy.

THE VICAR'S DAUGHTER

When you believe *Jesus—well,* that is a different thing! When you believe in HIS presence and promise, HIS power, HIS grace, and HIS strength, then you are marching on the victory highway toward the hills of answered prayer. As *you* decrease *He* must increase. The less of self, the more of Him. The more the crucifixion of the *self-life* with its spirit of pride, the more the resurrection rays of *His life* will impart power and health to *your* soul and body.

There is one meeting I shall *never* forget. It was held in the arena in Winnipeg some years ago. Assisting in the campaign was our dear friend, Archdeacon Fair, of the Anglican Church. He brought to the meeting one of his Vicars, a godly clergyman, named Hobbs. This dear brother had a daughter who had been sent home from the most famous clinic in America to die. There was no hope as far as man was concerned.

So the two reverend gentlemen. brought that woman to the meeting when she was in such excruciating pain that she was under the influence of opiates. She had to take them in order to live at all, for the suffering and pain was unendurable. She sat in a large chair—cushioned and surrounded by pillows. The rink was filled, not only with people, but with the presence of the Lord.

Toward the close of the service, I felt an unusual—but now familiar—feeling coming into my heart. I was literally melted in His Presence Divine. I turned to a minister sitting near and said, "The Lord is in this place and I think He is going to work a miracle tonight that will shake this meeting with the manifestation of His power." No sooner had I said those words, than *I felt an impartation of faith* for the sick woman. I did not delay. Stepping over to the side of Archdeacon Fair, I asked him to pray with me for the daughter of this Vicar. He grasped my hand and said, "My Brother, I can feel the presence of Jesus in this meeting in a way I have never felt Him before in all my life. I feel that He will work this miracle tonight."

He did! Upon the poor, weary, sick body of this girl, the Hand Divine was laid; and she rested in the Arms Everlasting. We could see the flush of health come back to her cheeks. She did not die. She lived, and she lives today as a living testimony to the power of our wonderful Lord.

A year later, when I visited that same building once again, I stood on the very spot where the Lord visited me that night. As I stood there, I remembered what I had been doing and what had happened at the moment He imparted to me the faith that my own poor heart lacked. That is why I say that faith is a *gift* of God. You do not possess it to use at will, but for the purpose for which He gives it and permits you to keep it.

Let me repeat. He gives us the necessary faith for all things that are in accordance with His blessed will. That faith is first *given* and then grows as a *fruit* of the Spirit. But for the mountain-moving faith that banishes disease and sweeps away all barriers by miraculous power, I still maintain that such faith is possible *only* when it is imparted and *that* when it is the Savior's will.

So, put *all* your trust in Jesus, for your help cometh *alone* from Him. Lean hard on the Master's breast, for only as you contact Him can you drink in the sweetness of His presence; and let not the devil deceive you into believing in the power of your *own* spiritual attainments—for without the Man of Calvary you can do *nothing*. Trust Him when faith is *withheld*, and *praise* Him when it is given. Remember that "He doeth all things well." You and I would blunder and err along the pathway, were it not for His restraining and withholding hand, as well as His bounteous provision for our every need. The things that seem good to you today, *could* wear the robes of sorrow in your tomorrows. How much better it is to let Him have *His* way with you, than to always try to have *your* way with Him.

That is my message. It is Jesus! Only Jesus. The Christ of Calvary who is the Giver of every good and perfect gift is also the Author and Finisher of your faith. Rejoice in the love that will not let you go! Be happy in the presence of a Friend who knows you better than you know yourself. Then some day when the toils of life are the greatest, you will sing:

"All the way my Savior leads me,
Cheers each winding path I tread;
Gives me grace for every trial,
Feeds me on the living bread.
Though my weary steps may falter,
And my soul athirst may be,
Gushing from the rock before me,
Lo, a spring of joy I see."

And what greater joy can there be than the possession of that faith which is The Faith of God!

10
Faith is a Fruit

CHRISTIAN EXPERIENCE IS a great adventure. We never arrive at the finality of that walk or experience. No matter what mountain peak we climb today, there is always another one to be climbed a little way ahead. The future is greater than the past, for there are Elysian fields and meadows of glory that have never been explored. It is this great truth that presents such a challenge to the follower of the Lord Jesus. Under His leadership—for He never drives or coerces—we are privileged to climb in spirit very near to the gates of a world that human eyes can not see; and are kept by the Peace of God which passeth all understanding, through Christ Jesus. It is then we begin to comprehend the incomprehensible, and to watch the apocalypse of the mysteries that are hidden to so many.

Of one thing, among many, the Bible speaks with no uncertain voice. It distinctly states that spiritual things are discerned only with the mind of the Spirit. The finite mind of man is incapable of understanding, not only the Infinite, but also the things that pertain to the Infinite. The reason for this is that they are two distinct and different realms. There is no gate that leads from one to the other, apart from the Lord Himself; and there is no method by which man has ever been able to understand or approach God, except though our Savior. He said of Himself, "I am the door; no man cometh to the Father but by me." If it were possible for man to enter the realm of the spiritual though the gateways of the mind and along the roads of the intellect, he would soon be building a Tower of Babel which would reach into the heavens; and the next thing you know, he would be *attempting* to dethrone God Himself. As a matter of fact, that is just what he has been trying to do. Nearly all of our modern philosophies, which are offering substitutes for the "old time religion", are attempting to humanize God and deify man. Thwarted in their attempt to understand the Infinite with their finite minds, they have sought to materialize all things which relate to the Spirit and which are connected with the power of God.

What has this done? Because of man's limited, finite understanding, he has attempted to turn "salvation by grace, through faith," into a salvation by conduct. He has sought to put the emphasis upon what he does rather than what he is. In his sight, therefore, character has become the "cross" upon which self is crucified and the baser instincts are doomed to writhe and twist but never die. As a result, the cross on which the Savior died becomes to him unnecessary and obsolete.

All this is of very great importance in the light of what I am now going to say. Why has natural man made faith a product of a finite mind, when all of the other fruits of the Spirit he has attributed to God? To many, many Christians, faith still is their own ability to believe a promise or a truth, and is often based on their struggles to drive away doubt and unbelief through a process of continuous affirmations.

Only the other day I heard a minister illustrating what faith is. He told us that it is a necessary factor in the development of every phase of our lives. In that I agreed—to some extent, at any rate. He said that when we get on a streetcar, we exercise faith. We have faith in the car, faith in the motorman, and faith in the power that will propel the vehicle along its tracks. He went into a multitude of departments connected with our everyday living, and used many homely illustrations in support of what he said were manifestations of our faith. He concluded with this question: "If we have faith in the motorman, should we not have faith in God?"

> *Have we not looked at a promise, and then struggled and striven with all our mental might to bring about the result by our own ability to believe?*

even related to it. To say that the "mountain-moving faith," of which Jesus spoke, is a grown-up brother of "faith in a motorman," is ludicrous to me.

No matter how much you nurture and culture the spirit that the world interprets as "faith", it will never grow into the *faith* that was introduced by Jesus in the days of long ago. Let us be honest! Have not we, also, tried to do that very thing? Have we not said, "I am going to believe that it is done, and if I can believe it is done, then it will be done?"

Some time ago a poor, deluded man, who undoubtedly loved his Lord, stuck his hand into a basket of snakes to prove his *faith* in God. For weeks he was sick, lingering between life

The faith of which he spoke was not New Testament faith at all. It was not and death. He came through all right, but it was a regrettable incident that did much to destroy the confidence of many in real Christian experience and a scriptural walk with God. He no doubt believed God; but what he called faith savored of sinful presumption.

One day some years ago, I had a long conversation with one of the secretaries of Pandita Ramabai who was a beloved spiritual leader in India. She told me the story of how the "cobras came to Mukti," following a wonderful and glorious visitation of the Blessed Holy Spirit upon the girls in the home and school. It was during the night that these cobras appeared and bit many of the girls in the compound. No doubt for a moment or two there was great fear; but so wonderfully did the Spirit of the Lord impart faith for the emergency, that instead of groans and cries of anguish, there arose to heaven a great shout of victory and praise. Not a girl died from the deadly bites! Every one was healed. The power of the Lord delivered them! It was the imparted faith of God that brought them through.

There is *belief* in faith, but *faith* is more than belief! There is a rock on the mountain, but the mountain is more than the rock. Should the rock assert that it is *the mountain,* then I would say to it, "You are presuming too much." The truth that should be emphasized is this: the ingredients of one's own mental manufacture cannot be mixed in spiritual, apothecaries' crucibles, and produce faith. A little more confidence, an extra pinch of trust mixed with a little stronger belief—plus a few other things—will not produce the faith that moves mountains. You are nearest the manifestation of this imparted grace when you realize your own helplessness and entire dependence upon the Lord!

THE LOVE OF GOD

Galatians 5:22 states that faith is a fruit of the Spirit. Is it not time we commenced to believe it? Look at the other gracious fruit growing on the tree of the blood-washed heart and life. First, there is love. Whose love is it with which we love? Is it our own love that has been made cleaner and sweeter because of something which has happened in our hearts? No, ten thousand times *no!* It is the love of God shed abroad in the heart by the Holy Ghost. It is God's wonderful love that fills the rooms of the heart; and only the possession of that Love Divine makes it possible for us to love our enemies.

When Stephen was stoned by cruel iniquitous men, what made him cry, 'lord, lay not this sin to their charge"? It was not said for effect! Neither was it an assumed expose of heroism in a moment of crisis. It was the love of God shed abroad in his heart by the Holy Spirit that enabled him to bless those who cursed him in genuine love for his murderers! The world might say it is ridiculous for a man to act like that; and ridiculous it is to an unregenerate heart —but not to the Christian—not to the redeemed who by grace have become partakers of the Divine Nature. It was real love—God's love bursting though the heart of Stephen, which flowed like a river from the Source of Grace. Was it not much like our Savior who spoke, in the sufferings of Calvary, "Father, forgive them, for they know not what they do"? It was love that caused Jesus to say that. God's love! It was the Love of Heaven in Jesus paying earth a little visit.

It was not by chance that both Stephen and Jesus said practically the same thing. Stephen was not trying to imitate his Master; neither was Jesus holding Himself up as only an example for men to struggle to emulate. The fact is that they both said the same thing because both had the same love. It was the love of God in both hearts. Jesus had it because He *was God;* Stephen had it because he *had God* in his heart.

Human love can be improved. It can be made better by increasing in quality and quantity; but if man were to live a million years he could never make it good enough to equal the love of God. How do we get God's love? God gives it, and the Spirit imparts it. Not only is this true of the *Love* of God but it is *also* true of the *Faith* of God.

JOY FROM THE HILLS

Then, we have joy! Joy is the second fruit of the Spirit mentioned by Paul in his letter to the Galatians. It is not the second in importance, but it is the second in the list of those graces that the Spirit cultivates and enables to grow in the heart of the blood-washed. What is this joy? Is it dependent upon environment and circumstance for its manifestation and expression? Do many other things have to be equal in order for it to work out in the realm of experience?

Some years ago I was a speaker in a camp meeting in a district in which many of the people were very, very poor. One night, just before time for 'the service, I drove down the road in my car to get away from people in order to have opportunity to meditate a little while before going into the pulpit to preach. In the modern automobile it does not take much time to cover the distance of a few miles, and soon I was five miles away from the camp. As I passed a wooded section, I saw a man and a woman with four children come out of the woods and start up the road. They were all barefooted. They were carrying their shoes in their hands; that is, those who were fortunate enough to

> *There is belief in faith, but faith is more than belief.*

possess shoes. Only the oldest child of the four children had shoes!

I stopped my car and hailed them. Smilingly, but with evident bashfulness, they accepted my offer to them of a ride. They were on their way to the camp meeting. At the gates of the camp they sat on the grass and put on their shoes. In just a few minutes they had traveled the three miles in my car that would have taken them over an hour to walk. The next night I *happened* to pass that way again, and gave them a ride. It so *happened* that I was in that vicinity every night, and asked them to ride with me to the services.

On the way, after the strangeness and bashfulness bad worn off, they would testify and sing, and sing and testify! Their joy was so abundant, that it was a tonic to my soul. It helped me to preach better! They carried their shoes to save the leather from wearing out on the concrete road. They were as poor as the proverbial turkey owned by Job and lived many, many miles back in the mountains; but they were richer by far than many who lived in great houses and who had more than enough of the possessions of this fleeting world.

One night, toward the end of the camp, I said to the father, "Perhaps, My Brother, the day will come when the Lord will give you a better and larger home. You know that He often prospers us temporally as well as spiritually. The Bible says that…" The brother interrupted me. A smile of happiness came across his face and he commenced to sing:

"A tent or a cottage, why should I care?
They're building a palace for me over there;
Though exiled from home, yet still I may sing,
All glory to God, I'm a child of the King."

The little folks helped him sing it, and his good wife sang it too. When he was finished, he scratched his matted hair on his old mountain-born head, and said, "Brother Price, you never need to tell me that I got to have a big house to make me happy. If the Lord gives it to me, then I will thank Him, but I have something in my heart I wouldn't sell for all the money in the world. It is the *joy* of the Holy Ghost."

That is what I mean. You cannot get up in the morning and say, "This is the day in which I will be full of joy. I am going to be very happy today, for I have made up my mind to have lots of joy." Either you have it, or you don't. The worldly man can have his synthetic joy that is the plaything of environment and the slave of circumstance. But the Christian can have *imparted* joy in the Holy Ghost, and rejoice in its manifestation under *every* condition of life. It is not dependent upon surroundings; nor is it the slave of circumstance. It is the gift of God!

PEACE, PERFECT PEACE

Then, there is peace. Oh, the sweetness of that beautiful peace which God implants in the hearts of all who love Him! What a wonderful day it was for the disciples when Jesus said, "My peace I give unto you!" It was not to be the peace that the world knows, for that peace is false, weak and flimsy, and can be lashed into a storm at any moment by the blowing of the winds of trouble.

The peace He gives passes all human understanding. It is so deep, that no surface troubles can ever affect it; so divine that no human hand can ever reach it to take it away; deep settled peace in the soul! It is the peace Jesus had when in His regal dignity He "held his peace" before the howling mob in the halls of Pilate.

Let me ask you (for it is necessary that we recognize and receive this truth). Let me ask you again: "Can *you* create that peace? Can *you* bring it about by a switch in mental attitude, or a change in outlook? Can you even so much as develop the Peace that He alone can give?" You and I know the answer! Just settle into the arms of love in the heart of the storm, and know:

"Peace, perfect peace, though sorrows surge around. On Jesus' bosom naught but calm is found."

> *He does not give faith as a plaything to be operated for our own undoing or contrary to His will.*

It is His peace, imparted by the Spirit. All we have to do is to receive it. That is the beauty of the Christ- centered life— a life that is hid with Christ in God.

So it is with faith. He does not give it as a plaything to be operated for our own undoing and in things otherwise contrary to His will. He knows my need. He knows yours, too; and He has given His promise that no good thing will He withhold from them who walk uprightly. So we rest in that promise; and abide in Him, even as He abides in us.

To know that He is present—that He understands and cares—this is sufficient for me to know the joy which springs eternal in the knowledge that all things work together for good to them that love God to them that are the called according to His purpose. Then shall we know the rest that comes from turning self-reliance into Christ-reliance, as we cast *all* our cares upon

Him.

In the development of His will in your
life, let me assure you that when faith is
needed, it will not be withheld; for
The Giver of every good and perfect gift
is the Author and Finisher of our faith.

.

11
The Vessel Made of Clay

Few people have realized the close affinity between the *natural* and the *supernatural*—*between* the *body* and the *spirit*. We have erroneously segregated the two, and have put them in realms so far apart that many think of the Lord as being able to meet only our spiritual needs. When that is as far as we go, we inevitably overlook the glorious, Blood-bought privileges that are ours for the physical man.

The great, redemptive work of our Lord covers the COMPLETE MAN—body, soul and spirit! It even reaches into the realm of physical necessities. Jesus said to his disciples, "Take no (anxious) thought, saying, 'what shall we eat?' or, 'what shall we drink?' or, 'wherewithal shall we be clothed?' for your heavenly

Father knoweth that ye have need of all these things. But seek ye first the kingdom of God, and His righteousness; and all these things shall be added unto you" (Matthew 6:31-34).

These are not inferential statements but direct and definite declarations. He not only said that our Heavenly Father knew we had *need* of these things, but definitely promised that He would *supply* them.

There is a very close link between the spiritual and the natural. His disciples were not to seek the natural, but instead to seek the spiritual. They were first to find the Kingdom and then, entering the Kingdom, they would find an abundance that would meet every need of their lives. That was the direct promise of our Lord!

Hundreds of years before Jesus came to this earth, one of the Prophets of God found himself away from any source of human supply—by a brook—and there God vindicated His Word to him by sending the ravens with his food in the gloaming of the morning and the evening. The widow's barrel of meal could not be emptied, because of her unlimited supply in His treasure store. He did not supply the meal because she sought it—but because she
OBEYED HIM!

The order has ever been "SEEK YE FIRST THE KINGDOM OF GOD!" That is why the emphasis is on the surrender of the natural to the spiritual, and our laying upon the altar the whole of our Adamic natures; that Christ might be to us spiritually, and then physically, all He has promised to be. The order of the Lord has always been CREATION and then "RE-CREATION". It has been first that which is NATURAL and, after that, that which is SPIRITUAL. In the 18th chapter of Jeremiah, we read, "The word which came to Jeremiah from the Lord, saying Arise and go down to the potter's house, and, there I will cause thee to hear My words. Then I went down to the potter's house, and, behold, he wrought a work on the wheels. And the vessel that he made of clay was marred in the hands of the potter: so he made it again another vessel, as seemed good to the potter to make it. Then the word of the Lord came to me saying, 'O house of Israel, cannot I do with you as this potter?' saith the Lord. 'Behold as the clay is in the potter's hand, so are ye in Mine hand, 0 House of Israel'" (Jeremiah 18:1-6).

It has never been the purpose of the Creator to do a "patched-up job!" The vilest of sinners become "NEW CREATIONS" when they put themselves in His hands. The disease may be of the flesh, but THE CURE IS OF THE SPIRIT! The broken clay must once again be put into the hands of the Eternal Potter, that He may make it again another vessel, as seemeth good to the Potter to make it!

A COMPLETE WORK

How many people come for healing, looking for a physical touch, only! They want the Lord to touch the *body*, whereas the Lord is longing to TOUCH THE SPIRIT! The physical manifestation will come; but God is a Spirit, and

> *His power operates from the inside out!*

the flow of the Resurrection Life must come though the Spirit primarily and not merely though the physical flesh. When Jesus said, "I came that ye might have Life and that ye might have it more abundantly"; He spoke not only of spiritual life, but of that life which would literally permeate every atom of our beings, and *saturate* us with the glory of the Life that knows no end.

There are those who come looking for healing, but not for the HEALER! They have anticipated physical thrills. Prayer in instances may have seemed to no avail; but no petition can ever be offered in vain, and unanswered prayer today does not necessarily mean it will go unanswered tomorrow. "Beloved, I wish above all things that thou mayest prosper and be in health, even as thy soul prospereth" (III John 2). The change *externally* is frequently superseded by the change internally— transformed by His Spirit in the *inner man* before the manifestation of the transformation is seen in the outer man! Certainly the scripture quoted, from the pen of the inspired John, throws a

Divine Light upon the subject. Here was prosperity for the complete man, but, that he should prosper and be in health was contingent upon the prosperity that was *within!*

That is why people who say, "If the Lord will heal me, I will serve Him as long as I live," are "putting the cart before the horse." They are looking for the manifestation of His power from the *outside* in, when in reality His power operates from the INSIDE, OUT! Our bodies are not only the *shells* in which we live; but they are the tabernacles, too, of the Most High! Does He not want them well and strong? The healing rays of His Resurrection Life do not shine upon us from the outside, but shine *through us from within.*

The law of the Lord is PROGRESSION! We are changed from glory to glory, but growth *toward* perfection is never *perfection* until the ultimate is reached. There is nothing perfect in the human, for perfection is found *only* in the Divine. We come to Him that we might have *Life,* and that we might have it more abundantly. His life! The Resurrection Life overflowing until we are inundated in its flow!

It is good when we sing, "Come To Jesus!" It is better when we say, "Jesus has come to me." It is richer by far, however, when we can declare, "He lives within my heart!" It is scriptural for people who are in need to seek out the elders and to call for prayer from the lips of some consecrated man, but it is not God's ultimate. *In Him* we need no priest, for *He* is indeed our High Priest. *In Him* we need no intermediary, for He is *The One Mediator* between God and man. The veil of the temple has been riven from top to bottom; and the Holy of Holies has been made accessible to all of Adam's race who, dying with Him in His substitutional death, will also rise with Him in the glory and power of His Resurrection Life!

Then it is we take the whole being to the ONE WHO MADE IT! We take it in consecration and surrender. We take it in yieldedness. Then the vessel that was made of clay is left in the keeping of the Heavenly Potter, who makes it yet another vessel after His pleasure!

Though it be broken, He throws it not away. With what tenderness and love does He reshape us, and impart Himself as our healing in body, soul, and spirit.

EATING WITHIN

It is not the evangelist nor yet the preacher who "saves". God may use an anointed man in the declaration of His truth, but no hands—other than the hands of the Lord Himself—ever bear the Blood of the Everlasting Covenant in its application to the human heart. The elders of the church may anoint with oil and lay on their hands in the name of the Lord Jesus. The minister may give the broken bread, and put to other lips the cup of communion; but that does not necessarily mean that the recipient receives the broken Body and the shed Blood of the Lord Jesus. The communicant must not only "eat the bread" and "drink the cup" of the Lord's Supper but must actually partake in *Spirit* of the Sacrifice of His Lord, in order to fulfill the true purpose of this most holy and precious Sacrament.

> *There is no formula for healing.*

There is no formula for healing; neither is there any formula or rule by which one can grow in grace. When we at last come to the end of self; when in condemnation of our fleshy natures—in contempt and disgust for the Adamic life which has brought us Spiritual sorrow and Physical pain—we fully yield ourselves, not merely our conduct but OURSELVES, to the Headship of our glorious Lord; then begins the LIFE SUPERNAL. It is not by imitation but by *participation* that we become of LIKE NATURE—LIKE SUBSTANCE, "because as He is, so are we in this world (I John 4:17).

This transformation so permeates the entire man, that suffering of the body goes in conjunction with the banishment of the pain and anguish of the heart; for whom the Son sets free, is free indeed!" (John 8:36). His transforming glory is reflected in us as we, ourselves, are changed from glory to glory, until we shall AWAKE IN HIS BLESSED LIKENESS!

Did not our Lord say, "Go and sin no more, lest a worse thing befall thee? Over and over again He tied up external disease with the condition of the inward man. He did not say, "How sick are you?" or "How much does it hurt?" but "Do you believe? Have you living faith within?" He was not concerned with the condition of the exterior, but He always probed beneath the "proud flesh" into the condition of the interior. Instead of struggling and striving to bring about healing by this prescribed process, or by that, it is much more pleasing—and infinitely more effective—to place the vessel back in the hands of the Maker.

The human is ever prone to overemphasize little things and neglect the greater for the lesser. Where we eat and sleep, as well as other earthly matters, may receive Divine guidance, but they are *not* the ULTIMATE with God. He wants us to know *Him,* whom to know *aright* is Life eternal. He wants to lead us into Heavenly realms. So many of us are concerned about the *geographical* aspect of our obedience. "Shall I go to this town, Lord?" "Shall we live here, or shall we live there?" It may be perfectly true that the Lord has a definite *place* for us, but it is of far more *importance* that WE LIVE IN THE SPIRIT! With Jesus, the supreme thing was, not whether He was in Judea or in Samaria, but that He was in the *center* of His Father's Will.

MY HOME IS GOD

One of old asked Him, "Master, where dwellest Thou?" Jesus replied, "Come and see." It was so relatively unimportant, however, that no record was kept of the location of the dwelling place of Jesus. We do not know just where He was staying. The street was not given, nor was the number of the house. Was it in the city, or was it in the countryside? Perhaps it was beneath the outstretched arms of some forest tree, for we are told that He had not where to lay His head. We do not know *where;* but we do know that HIS HOME WAS GOD! He came to do the *Father's* Will; and the Father's Will was *His* Will! We do know that He lived in the place of IMPLICIT OBEDIENCE, "for though He were a Son, yet learned He obedience by the things which He suffered"; (Heb.) "and being found in fashion as a man, He humbled Himself, and became obedient unto death, even the death of the cross." (Phil. 2:8). Shall we not also say then that sometimes *our* suffering comes to lead us into the place of obedience? If that be so, should not we seek our *Healer* rather than our healing?

It may be human for us to deal with the *effects,* and to constantly look upon and pray for *them,* but it is not as pleasing to our Father as to ask for grace TO EXAMINE THE CAUSE. That is why *what* we *are* is far more important than what we *do.* "I will lift up mine eyes unto the hills! From whence cometh my help?" (Psalm121). Certainly it is not from the hills! "MY HELP COMETH FROM THE LORD WHICH MADE HEAVEN AND EARTH!"

We read about faith that will move mountains, and immediately begin to look at the *mountains,* instead of seeking the faith which will *move* them. He is the Author and the Finisher of our faith! If He *begins* it, and it *ends* in Him, why should we struggle to *manufacture* it, when He alone can impart faith! Oh, how sweet is His lovely Presence, and how marvelous— beyond description— is the exercise of HIS FAITH and the manifestation of HIS POWER. In ourselves, we can do nothing! Absolutely nothing!

We are so cluttered up with attending to the *external* details, and so weary in our unceasing toil, that we fail to hear the *voice* of Jesus say, "Come unto Me and rest! Lay down, thou weary soul, lay down, Thy head upon My breast!" It is then that we discover it is not *our* faith in Him, but *HIS FAITH* operating *in us.* It is not by the *might* of our prayer, nor by the powerful *thundering* of our entreaties, but by the beautiful moving of *His Holy Spirit.* One of His dear children who had been healed in body, soul, and spirit, and who was a living miracle of the recreative power of our Lord, said "It was when I STOPPED that JESUS STARTED!" How blessed it is to come to the place where we say, "I cannot, but HE CAN!"

Become *released unto God!* Just LET HIM! He spoke the Word—and a Universe was born! He said 'let' and the oceans were in their places! He spoke and the stars were in the firmament! All was done at His command. He has *always* been Sovereign! He is *that* today! He is calling upon His children for a *complete* relinquishment of *all* that they have, and *all* that they are! Then as the darkness moves out, THE LIGHT MOVES IN! As *self goes,* HE COMES! From within us there *then* begins to flow the "Rivers of Living Water"—healing streams in the desert of our lives. The wilderness, which *we* are, begins to rejoice; and the desert, which we have been, is made to blossom as the *Rose!*

12
Living Waters

AFTER THE HEAT and toil of the day, we find rest and repose in sleep. It is out of that sleep we awaken with renewed strength for the tasks that lie ahead. It is out of death *also* that we awaken! It was said of our glorious Lord, "Except a corn of wheat fall into the ground and die, it abideth alone; but if it die, it bringeth forth much fruit" (John 12:24).

It was out of His death that the glorious harvest of Eternal Life blossomed! He Himself became the FIRST-FRUITS of them that slept. Without death, there can be no Resurrection. He does not impart His resurrection life to us because we *live* for Him; but because, for His sake, we are willing to *die* and allow *Him* to live His Resurrection life in *us*.

God saw that the human race could not be Divinely indwelt in its fallen state; lest in eating of the Tree of Life man would live forever in his fallen condition. *Death had to come.* The royal edict had gone forth, "The soul that sinneth, it shall die." It was only in the new creation that Christ could indwell His people, or the Spirit of God take up His abode again within the confines of the entity called "man". So the typical sacrifices of the Old Testament, and the antitypical Sacrifice offered, once and for all, of the New Testament took us not only into death—but through death—to the power of His resurrection!

It was vicariously that He suffered for us on the Cross of Calvary. It was substitutionally that He died upon the accursed Tree. He took us with Him to the Cross and then He took us from the Cross into His grave; and, through the grave, we went with Him to the dawning of the first Easter morning, and the warm, eternal glow of His Resurrection Life. Positionally, we are now seated with Him in heavenly places, for we are in Him, even as He is in us, the Christ!

At the time of His first advent, there was no room for Him in the inn. His pre-incarnate glory had filled the heavens; and yet, when he was to take upon Himself the form of man and, through the Miracle of the Incarnation, be born of a virgin mother, there was found no room for Him in the inn. You see, there was no room, because the rooms were already occupied! Even so, in these days, at the time of His advent as the Indwelling Christ, who will make our bodies His temples and will Himself tabernacle within these vessels of clay; if the rooms are occupied, He will find no place within to take up His abiding!

If only we could realize that His coming will bring life, light and health, we would not be so preoccupied with giving place to our selfish, fleshly desires and purposes so that He is crowded out. He who bore our sicknesses and our sorrows would come to give us His peace, rest and joy.

When He comes, will He find faith in the earth? One step further—will He find faith in the "earth" which *we* are? If we would become less concerned about what we do, forget our petty bickerings about Biblical interpretations, and open wide the gates of our beings to let the King of Glory in, we would start once again the music of joy by the angel choirs of the glory-world. All heaven would rejoice in such a surrender as that! *Do you believe Him enough to make room for Him?*

FROM THE INSIDE OUT

He does not come as a postman, bringing gifts from the Father, leaving them at our door, and then walking away!

Some people would use the Bible like a mail-order catalog. They ask the Father to give them what they want, and then expect the angelic messengers to bring them this, or to bring them that; in order that their own desires might be gratified, and their needs met in the way they want them to be. The light, which Christ brings, does not shine from the outside in; but it radiates from the

> *The gifts He imparts, He administers and operates.*

INSIDE OUT! The gifts He imparts, He administers and operates. He does not literally "give" light. He *is* the Light! He does not impart health. He *is* the Health. It is the constant acknowledgment of His indwelling—the recognition that the life we now live in the flesh, we live *by the faith of the Son of God*, who gave Himself for us, and who now dwelleth within us—that brings us into vital union with Him. Room is made within us, BY THE SPIRIT, for the Incoming Christ! Commensurate with our surrender and our death to self, His light, His life, and His love permeate every department of our being! Perhaps the transformation, at first, is spiritual only. Possibly the transformation is brought about by the operation of the Spirit within our spirit, bringing us light, understanding, and the deep settled peace which always floods the life when He dwells within.

Following this experience of His grace, manifested within our lives, the cup of His mercy overflows and the *physical body* begins to feel His Resurrection Life!

Instead of struggle, it is REST. Instead of agonizing, it is PEACE. The consciousness that Christ is dwelling within, and that He has taken the government upon His own shoulders, brings us into a blessed quietness before the Lord. How many times, if only we could hear His Voice, upon our ears in gentlest tones would fall: *"Be still and know that 1 am God."*

One might say, "Yes, I believe that!" It is not enough to *believe* "that". Our troubles in days gone by has been just "that". We have accepted the *doctrine* as truth, when He is calling upon us to accept HIM as the TRUTH. It is not enough merely to "know" that in Christ is health, virtue, and saving power. We need to be INDWELT BY HIM! He does not *impart* virtue, separate from Himself. The miracle of healing is *never* separate from the Healer.

When our poor, diseased bodies and lives are transformed, it is only that our darkness is SWALLOWED UP IN HIS LIGHT! He—as our Health—overcomes our sickness. He—as our Strength—absorbs all our weakness. We are STRONG *IN HIM* for He does not, in the final analysis, make *us* strong, but He gives us *His* Strength. His Presence does it. We don't. There is LIFE in Jesus and in none other! Christ and Adam will not be joint tenants. Before the Second Adam will move in, the first Adam must move out. When the Light comes, the darkness is dispelled.

THE GREAT PHYSICIAN

When sickness visits homes, many call for a physician who comes to the house and diagnoses the case. The first thing the doctor does is to find out, if he can, what the difficulty is. When he arrives at his conclusion, he prescribes the remedy. It is the *remedy* for which the patient waits. The doctor is only a *means* to the remedy. He takes out a little pad of blanks, writes down a prescription, and someone goes to the drugstore to return with some little, black pills—or whatever the prescribed remedy might be. The confidence of the patient is in the remedy. The sufferer looks for the efficacy to be in the pills. The faith and trust the patient places in the doctor goes only so far as to hope that he knows the remedy; and that he knows what he is doing when he writes the prescription. When the little pill is taken, however, the patient settles back and waits for the pill to do its work.

How different it is with the Lord Jesus! The virtue is not in what *He prescribes;* it is not in doing this, or in doing that. It is not even in knowing "how to receive healing"; but it is the PERSON of the Lord Jesus Christ, Himself. He sees us in our sick and sinful state of impurity. He knows *the only remedy is holiness.* We have read that, too, and have made the mistake of *struggling* to become holy. There is no such thing as holiness apart from *Him.* He does not leave holiness at the door of our hearts, and then move away and ask *us* to utilize it in the living of our lives!

> *The virtue is not in doing this, or in doing that. It is not even in knowing "how to receive healing." It is the PERSON of the Lord Jesus Christ, Himself.*

We go to the altar and pray for sanctification and sometimes jump to our feet and say, "Praise the Lord, the work is done." However, He does not *give* sanctification to anyone. *HE* IS OUR SANCTIFICATION. When His sanctification overflows our lives, we are truly sanctified in Him! "But of Him are ye in Christ Jesus, who of God is made unto us wisdom, and righteousness, and sanctification, and redemption: that, according as it is written, He that glorieth, let him glory in the Lord" (1 Cor. 1:30,31).

Even so in Divine Healing, we do not *take* a "pill." We do not prescribe to the patient: "Now you must do this, and you must do that, and then the Lord will touch you with healing power." It is not a question of being made right in our *own* righteousness, or ready with our own *readiness,* for in James 5:15 we read, "and if he have committed sins,they shall be forgiven him." What the poor, broken sufferers need, in all their unworthiness—and even in their sin, is to come in absolute surrender to the Lord—to LET JESUS IN!

It is not what He *gives*—*but* what He *is!* He is *Resurrection Life!* He *is* Wisdom! *He* is Righteousness! He *is* Healing! As He once led captivity captive, He will do it again in you and in me! As, in the days of old, virtue flowed from Him into the woman who had an issue of blood—so once again—we too can feel the healing warmth of that glorious flow. The virtue is not in what we do *for* Him. It does not go from us *to* Him. IT FLOWS FROM HIM THROUGH US!

OUR VICTORY

This is the reason then that there must, of necessity, be death to self. There must be the acknowledgment of His Lordship and Headship. In Adam— before the Fall —there was Eternal Life. God created him—a Living Soul! When Adam severed his connection with the Author of Life, he fell under the sentence of death; and the Supreme Sacrifice became necessary to pay the penalty for sin and death. Our Blessed Lord chose to take upon Himself the form of man and to take the whole of humanity, which lay under the Adamic Curse, with Him into death—even the death of the Cross. Down He went into Hell; but then He ascended up on high—into glorious Resurrection Life! Having consummated this tremendous Redemptive work, the cry went ringing through the islands and continents for men to turn from their sinful ways and to BELIEVE INTO THE LORD JESUS CHRIST! Accepting Him as their Savior, they were saved! Acknowledging Him as their Redeemer, they enter into Redemption. He took their death into His grave with Him and, coming forth triumphant from the darkened tomb, His voice rang forth— echoing down the corridors of time:

"I AM THE RESURRECTION AND THE LIFE: HE THAT BELIEVETH IN ME, THOUGH HE W E R E DEAD, YET SHALL HE LIVE: AND

WHOSOEVER LIVETH AND BELIEVETH IN ME SHALL NEVER DIE."

To obtain Resurrection Life, we must "believe" in order to *receive* HIM. We cannot have Resurrection Life *apart* from Him! Obedience to New Testament *precepts* will no more avail than obedience to the Law of Moses. Neither will wearing out our shoe leather, doing this or doing that, prevail! It is only by **RECEIVING CHRIST!** That is the great fundamental! It is the eternal essential! There is *no* other way. We must receive *Him!* If we receive Him, the self-life has to go; for there *cannot be two headships in the one body.* A two-headed creature is always a monstrosity; and there would be endless confusion, and ultimate despair, with two contradictory governments.

When the surrender of self is made, and we enthrone Christ as the Captain of our Salvation, no longer does the Child of Redemption cry, "Soul, thou hast much goods laid up for many years; take thine ease, eat, drink, and be merry"; but rather, "For me to live is Christ!" and "I am crucified with Christ: nevertheless I live; yet not I, but Christ liveth in me: and the life which I now live in the flesh I live by THE FAITH OF THE SON OF GOD, who loved me, and gave Himself for me." Then comes the flow and surge of that glorious Life Divine. It is not a struggle. It is Rest. It is Strength. It is Healing; as well as Power. Not the power of destructive explosive—but the irresistible power of His Life and Joy and Peace.

> *We are merely the riverbed and His life is the river.*

People foolishly imagine that they have to strive and strain, groan and importune; to measure up to a life in the high-calling of God in Christ Jesus, our Lord! Does a river struggle to roll down hill? Does its water strive and strain as it gently flows on to where the great arms of the sea are opened wide to receive it?

We are merely the riverbed, and *His Life*

is the river. He flows through us, constantly giving, imparting, radiating, and infusing; until our very lives are HID WITH CHRIST IN GOD! Our natures are transformed by His glorious Nature Divine! Our sicknesses, our sufferings, and our pain—can they maintain their grip and hold in the warm flow of His Love Divine?

In God's deliverance, we find that He can be severe, as well as loving; but in His severity there is always love! He will not allow us to take shortcuts; but His command is: "SLAY UTTERLY!" There is no other way. The surrender must not be partial; it must be UN-CONDITIONAL! In ALL—ALL—our ways, would we acknowledge Him, that He may direct our paths! If we do it just for convenience, or to receive healing, is it any wonder that the thing for which we pray is so many times withheld?

Doctors do not delight in cutting into "proud flesh" but must remove it entirely before healing virtue will come to any wound in the body. In dealing with the woman who came from the coasts of Tyre and Sidon, superficial thinking might declare that Jesus dealt rather cruelly with her! His words must have pierced her deeply, and one would naturally expect she would be wounded in her spirit because of what He said. But when we look further into what He did, we find that His seeming severity was baptized in love and impregnated with His loving kindness and tender mercy! We find that there are no shortcuts in ridding ourselves of the Adamic nature, in order that the Divine nature might come forth!

THE WAY TO VICTORY

Beneath the outstretched arms of the trees in the Garden, our Lord cried, "IF it be possible, let this cup pass from Me." And then, in complete abandonment of Himself to God and to the purpose and will of His Father, He finished, "Nevertheless, not My will but Thine be done." The only way to The Resurrection was through The Garden.

The only way to His victory over the tomb was by the way of the Cross; and He has to bring us to that place! "Because I live," said He, "Ye too shall live"; but we know full well that His resurrection life in us must be preceded by our death!

Even the *seemingly* good side of our Adamic nature has to be sacrificed with the *acknowledged* bad. Isaac was the son of promise, yet he had to be "sacrificed" in obedience to God's command. Can you not hear the heart-cry of that adoring father—wrung from the very depths of his being? Was not Isaac his child of promise? And yet, the Lord had said, "Slay him upon the altar of sacrifice." Slay his "good" Isaac! Slay even the child of promise! But here was the man who believed God, and IT WAS ACCOUNTED UNTO HIM FOR RIGHTEOUSNESS, for he took that good, living sacrifice and climbed with him to the top of the mountain. It was in, and through, his obedience that the revelation came! The RAM IN THE THICKET was revealed! It was the revelation of a SUBSTITUTE, provided by God and therefore acceptable unto Him. It opened wide the door to an experience which is so stupendous that only the Holy Spirit can reveal it to us, individually, with all its eternal implications.

The redemptive plan of our Blessed Lord, to cleanse humanity for His indwelling, is not by some "get-well-quick" system! Even as there are "quack doctors" who advertise their potions in magazines and papers and who promise recovery for stipulated amounts, within a specified time; so there are also pseudo-religious leaders who have devout ways and systems of divine healing so called, devised in other than God's way, but promising to bring relief. There is only one way! That way is CHRIST! Many times in history we have found confusion of tongues and the babble of voices as demagogues have cried this and proclaimed that! The Tower of Babel is not the only place where such confusion reigned!

THE LIVING WAY

In the days of Jesus' earthly walk, the Pharisees cried, "Lo, here is truth!" and the Sadducees, in contradiction said, "No, it is here." Grecian philosophers had long proclaimed that they had the truth. However, our Blessed Lord silenced them *all* in His declaration, "I am the Way, the Truth, and the Life. No man cometh unto the Father but by Me." There is no difference today. He *is* our Way. He is our *Truth.* *He* is our Life! There is no other way! There is no other Life! There is no other Truth! It is all very well to sing,

"Jesus shall reign where'er the sun, doth his successive journeys run..."

That is true to a degree, and the day is not far away when it will be gloriously fulfilled! But above and beyond that, our hearts should be continuously singing:

"Christ liveth in me. Christ liveth in me.! Oh! What a Salvation this—that Christ liveth in me!"

Flesh dies; and the Adamic nature must be crucified. It may hurt a bit to come to complete surrender, but that is where our Lord would bring us in Spirit and in Truth before He Himself can conde-

> *What a privilege it is to surrender, to lay our all at the Master's feet!*

scend to indwell this vessel of clay. One under testing has been heard to cry, "I cannot bear this cross!" The Voice Divine responded, "Do you want Me to take this cross away?" Understanding, super-naturally quickened, revealed that if it were removed a harder cross, and perhaps one to which she was not accustomed, might be substituted; so she did not ask for its removal. In a short time, however, there came the same, sweet Voice, "NOW, COMMIT IT UNTO ME." Then, with the committing, the light broke! The glorious light of revelation that God Himself was RISING TO TAKE ACTION! Underneath, the Everlasting Arms were lifting—lifting—lifting; and with the surge of that Resurrection Life, the *Cross* became a CROWN!

What a privilege it is to surrender! How blessed it is to be invited to lay our all at the Master's feet! How poor our understanding—in comparison with His!

How faulty our Adamic wills are in the light of the Divine Will that was fulfilled in Christ Himself. Beloved, there can be no short cuts! The inspired Word declares that if any man try to climb up any other way, the same is a thief and a robber; for the Lord Jesus Christ is the *only* door to God! No man can come to the Father but by Him! How sweet it is to reminisce as well as testify:

"I've found a Friend, Oh, such a Friend!
He loved me e'er I knew Him!
He drew me with the chords of love, And thus
He bound me to Him!"

We love to speak—doctrinally—about the Father seeing *us* in Christ; but to my heart is whispered the truth that He would first see *Christ in us.*

13
The Living Word

Before Jesus was born in Bethlehem of Judea, godly men of old looked to the Written Word. So it was that God revealed Himself in supernatural ways to a chosen few, in order that they might write the inspired Scriptures for others to read and walk by the light of the Written Word thus given. The day came when the WORD WAS MADE FLESH and dwelt among us! As the written Word was the THOUGHT of God, so the Living Word became the EMBODIMENT OF THAT THOUGHT, expressed through the Miracle of the Incarnation, in the Person of our Lord and Savior, Jesus Christ!

That is why every throbbing, vital statement, which left the lips of Jesus, was impregnated with this truth:

"I AM COME THAT THEY MIGHT HAVE LIFE, AND THAT THEY MIGHT HAVE IT MORE ABUNDANTLY" (John 10:10).

The words He spoke were SPIRIT AND THEY WERE LIFE! He was the "true Light which lighteth every man that cometh into the world:" (John 1:9), for "God is light, and in Him is no darkness at all;" (I John 1:5) and those who follow Him shall not walk in darkness, but shall have the LIGHT OF LIFE!

We have read what He said, and counted it beautiful! We have read about what He did, and have called it wonderful! We have—but, Oh, that our eyes might *see* the divinely appointed purpose of His ministry and that we might embrace with our hearts the fullness of His redeeming grace! The written word can never be read aright without the revealing light of the Living Word—The Word made flesh. The Word that came once to live AMONG us now has come to dwell WITHIN us!

Happy that day for us when in the history of eternity God reached up to the four corners of the realms supernal—infinite and eternal—and caught all of the glory, all of the grace, all of love, mercy, and truth, and then by the miracle of the Incarnation, He wrapped them all up together and put them in a virgin mother's arms in a bundle of pink babyhood and called His name JESUS, for He was to save a lost world from its sins!

He is our Life. He is our Healing. He is our strength. Not the word of the printed page; not our faulty interpretations of that written word; but the WORD MADE FLESH—THE LIVING WORD—The Word of God which once dwelt among us, but now is the Living Word who dwells within us! It is the Word which He is, and which we too can become, as He lives within; for by the flow of His life divine we are changed from glory to glory. When we *awake*, we will be in *His likeness!*

Many have taken a few of His sentences and built marvelous sermons around them. He has become, to a great extent, an Ideal—a Pattern for our living, and an Example for our conduct. Now that is all very well as far as it goes, but it certainly misses the mark of the high calling of God in Christ Jesus. What He said was a divine revelation of what He *is*. The things that He said and did were only the outward manifestations, the effulgent glory of the great dynamic cause, which He Himself is.

Paul did not cry for wisdom to know more *about Him;* but from the hungry depths of his innermost being, he cried: count all things but loss...that I may *know Him,* and the power of His resurrection!" It is this VITAL UNION with Christ that is necessary in our lives. We must *stop* our struggling to become "like Him." There is no need to spend long hours reading the biography of a king when you are, at last, in his royal presence!

The woman by Samaria's Wayside Well was greatly concerned as to which mountain it was, in which they were to worship God. Was it in the mountains of Jerusalem, according to the Jews; or in the mountains of Samaria, as contended by the Samaritans? Jesus saith

unto her, "The hour cometh when ye shall neither in this mountain, nor yet at Jerusalem, worship the Father... the hour cometh, and now is, when the true worshippers shall worship the Father in spirit and in truth; for the Father seeketh such to worship Him. God is a Spirit; and they that worship Him must worship Him in spirit and in truth."

HE IS OUR LIFE!

He Himself is the Way. He Himself is the Truth. He Himself is the *Life!* It is not the mental understanding, or the intellectual approbation of this fact, which brings joy unspeakable to the heart of the Christian. It is the EXPERIMENTAL realization of it that floods our spirits with the unleashing of His divine power and life. It is the flooding of the spirit of lives surrendered to Christ with the Light of the World, Himself!

All creation is groaning for its promised liberation! For the earnest expectation of the creature waiteth for the manifestation of the Sons Of God...the creature itself shall be delivered from the bondage of corruption into the glorious liberty of the children of God (Romans 8:19–23).

When at last our pitchers have been broken, his light will shine forth more gloriously than the light of the noonday sun! It will be the revelation of the Light of the World, which is Jesus, manifested through the lives of His surrendered and yielded children!

Time was when the presence and power of God was symbolized by a wooden ark. That day has gone. The *Lord* has written His law within our *hearts*. The Incarnate Christ has been enthroned in the lives of the children of obedience.

The shout is already beginning to well up from within, and when at last the cry goes forth, the walls of the Jericho of this world will come tumbling down! Just as there was amazement and consternation on the faces of the inhabitants of Jericho, so the world will stand in wonder and amazement at the manifestation of the Sons of God! The manifestation is not of *them;* it is of Christ! The written Word proclaims it, and every type and shadow declares it! The ancient prophet saw it by inspiration, as through a telescope, and spoke in clear and plain language of the triumph of the Lord, and the glory of the manifestation of the Sons of God. John, the Revelator, saw it as he was in the Spirit on the Lord's Day, on the lonely Isle of Patmos. The revelation, which burns within the spirit of man, infinitely surpasses any glory or manifestation borne without, for it is from within that the light shines! God Himself is His own interpreter, and He is making it plain!

> *The promises concerning Jesus include not only what He would do, but also what He would be.*

The promises, concerning Jesus, include not only what He would *do,* but also what He would *be.* The miracle of His grace is not merely what He would do *for* us, but what HE WOULD BE-COME *IN US.* It would have been wonderful, indeed, had He come to show us a plan whereby we could *find* Salvation, but it is unspeakably precious when we realize HE DIED TO *BE-COME* THAT SALVATION! Could a man receive Salvation and refuse the Savior? Is there such a thing as Christianity, without Christ? Could one ever be spiritual, without the Spirit? That is why our ecclesiastical rituals avail us nothing; though man has made them substitutes for His lovely, indwelling presence, and has tried to find sanctuary for his wounded spirit within the ceremony. He has oftentimes thereby closed the door against the entrance of the King of Glory!

One truth, which stands out in bold relief in the ministry and life of our Lord, is the privilege of progression and growth in grace and in the knowledge of the things of God! The Apostle Paul, in whose spirit the Living Christ was dwelling, proclaimed the same glorious truth, and admonished us *to go on to maturity.* That maturity is not the development of human understanding;

neither is it an increase in our intellectual knowledge concerning prophecy. It is, however, the *unhindered outflow of the knowledge of Christ Himself,* giving us understanding of the heart commensurate with our spiritual ability to *receive Him.*

The growth of the Christian life is, in reality, the increasing manifestation of HIS LIFE. As in the natural world the identity of the bride becomes lost in the bridegroom, so it is with the Bride of Christ! She literally becomes a partaker of the Divine Nature. "He that believeth in (into) Me, out of his innermost being shall flow rivers of Living Water." The surge of this Divine Flow of Resurrection Life will cover body, soul and spirit; and the Divine virtues of our adorable Lord will nullify and abrogate absolutely everything we have received under the Curse of the Law. This provision includes HEALING. It means *more* than HEALING; it is the *perpetuation* of HEALTH! It means the continuous operation in us of the DIVINE LIFE.

CHRIST IS ALL

Oh, that the sheep of His pasture, so cruelly beaten about by the forces of circumstance and environment, could once again hear the voice of the Good Shepherd, saying, "Come unto Me!" What an innumerable host of cults surround us, and with what insistence do they proclaim their dogmatisms and their private interpretations! Divine healers advertise their wares; and this method and that method are sold, until the atoning sacrifice of our Lord is well nigh measured out in classes and treatments—as if men could sell the sunlight by the bottle-full! Is not one fairly bewildered with the multitude of contentious voices which sound on every hand and side, in proclamation of this or of that virtue!

In the days of old, what demands the Pharisees and Sadducees placed upon the people before they would be accepted by the powers that be! They were required to give tithes where it could be proved that they had given. They must pray in public. They must do this and they must not do that. With legalisms they bound them and with chains of ritualism they enslaved them. But when Jesus came, He swept aside their traditional belief. He upset the "apple-cart" of their preconceived and pre-established prejudices. He showed His disdain for their Sabbath laws and healed men, because they needed His touch, whether it be on this day or on that. His tender appeal was directed to the hearts and spirits of the Suffering, the Sinful, and the Oppressed! "Come unto Me!" He said. That was all. They were to lay their heads upon His breast. There was no need to go through this gate or that door, for there was only one Door, after Jesus came. There was only one Way. There was only one Life. There was only One Salvation, and that was in the Savior! Directly they came to Him, there flowed from Him—into them—from His illimitable fountains of virtue. Life, Health, Strength, Joy and Peace! He was their Everything! They needed nothing beside Him. Whether one be a self-righteous Nicodemus or a poor, broken Mary of Magdala, He was the illimitable Source of Eternal Supply, and in Him they found all their need!

How intellectual we have tried to be! With what dignified phrases and meaningless platitudes have we shrouded the Person of our Blessed Lord! Then with what seeming cleverness and ingenuity have we dug our own wells, only to find that the waters were "Marah" (bitterness) and never did satisfy. We have builded us broken cisterns and, lo, their waters failed!

In the "far country" no prodigal can ever comprehend the sweetness of the rest and peace we enjoy in the Father's House. To let a man stay in the pigsty, though we give him an encyclopedia and textbooks on "How to be Happy, Well, Good, etc.," will never lift him out of the stench of his surroundings, nor bring to his innermost being the peace which he, in his heart, craves! Neither will it do him any good to sit in submission, listening to lectures on the beauty of the world outside, intermingled with a little, vehement scolding because he has gotten himself into the predicament which is his.

Jesus surrendered to the will of God for you; and now you may surrender absolutely to the will of the Father through Him!"

No, there is only one thing! He, as well as you and I, must determine within the heart and declare, "I will arise and go to my Father!" Then like the woman who, having an issue of blood, pressed through the throng to the side of her Lord, we must push aside people with their jargon of contending voices, as we crowd our way through this group and that, until we stand face to face with Eternal Peace—The Lord Jesus Christ Himself! The sunlight from His lovely face warms the heart, and the doors of our Spirit swing open to let "The Light Of The World" stream in!

AS MANY AS RECEIVED

He says, "Give Me your poor, broken, wasted life, and in return I will give you Mine. Give Me your weakness— battered and bruised by man's inhumanity to man and the cruelty of sinful circumstance—give it to Me, and I will give you My Courage, My Strength, and My Power! I died that you might live; and now as you die to all that is self, I live in you! I surrendered to the Will of God, for you; and now you may surrender—absolutely and completely—to the Will of the Father through Me!"

We left God in disobedience (in Adam all die) and we return in obedience (in Christ shall all be made alive). We come back into the direct care and keeping of the Creator—our Maker! In God's glorious and eternal Ultimate—in the Land of Endless Day—there will be no need of the sun, neither of the moon, for the Lamb Himself is the Light thereof! The Light that illumines heaven is the Light which illumines the Spirit. We should be seeking—not the "lime-light", but the Light.

In the final analysis, we can throw out—or otherwise push aside most of the things we have been taught to do— do—do! Why strive we to light our little candles when the sun is brightly shining? Why try we to push the ocean back, when our Heavenly Father has ordained that the force of gravity and the pull of the moon shall do that with consummate ease? It is the acknowledged Will of God that His sheep not wander about in blind superstition, seeking first this and then that as a source of healing. It is His desire that each of His little ones come into direct contact, and live in union with the Christ; that all may come to the Father.

Yet—how pitiful appears the account! He came unto His own and His own received Him not. He is the Light that shineth in darkness; and the darkness comprehendeth it not. He was the fulfillment of every prophetic utterance, and yet the students of the prophecies did not recognize Him. He called to people in need, but they turned deaf ears to Him and followed after superstitions and fables. He offered Himself, a Ransom for many; but He was despised and rejected of men—a Man of Sorrows and acquainted with grief.

Is it any wonder that He stood beneath the outstretched trees of Bethphage and cried, "O, Jerusalem, Jerusalem, thou that killest the prophets, and stonest them which are sent unto thee, how often would I have gathered thy children together, even as a hen gathereth her chickens under her wings, and ye would not! Behold, your house is left unto you desolate. For I say unto you, Ye shall not see Me henceforth, till ye shall say, Blessed is He that cometh in the name of the Lord" (Matt. 23:37-39).

In their blind ignorance and superstition they knew not what He said, let alone what He meant. He spoke of the Bread which He was, and all they could think about was the manna which fell from heaven on the burning sands of the wilderness centuries ago. He spoke of Rivers of Living Water—the Water that He Himself was—but they could visualize nothing beyond the pouring of some water from a pool upon a pile of stones they called an altar. How like man—even today-he would do anything

but simply RECEIVE HIM!

THE WELL OF GLORY

Receiving *Him* means giving up to Him the right to the right of one's self! The heart that opens to the REIGN OF THE CHRIST enters into the reality of His Presence. It is, as it were, that in the heart the lion and the lamb lie down together. We walk with Him in Heavenly places. He speaks, and the sound of His voice is so sweet, that the birds hush their singing! The living, pulsating reality of His Divine Indwelling springs up within our innermost being like an artesian well of heavenly glory! It is effortless; it just FLOWS. It permeates every fiber of the nature; and we do not have to wait until the Gates of Pearl unfold before we are lost in wonder, in love, and in praise!

As the human spirit runs up the flag of unconditional surrender, the flesh capitulates, and the Lord of Life is Sovereign. Christ is all, and in all; and throughout our being all that Christ *was*, He now becomes *in* us! We drink of His Life, His Healing, His Saving

Grace, and His Strength. His perfect Love has cast out all fear, and we learn to *know HIM as* the Only Wise God, the true mediator between God and men, the man Christ Jesus!

It is in Him we find our completeness; and we turn from agonizing, imploring petitioning to the realization that in finding Him is not only Life and Peace, but that it also brings the continuous assurance that he, in whom dwelleth this Christ of God, knows His felicity, bliss, and heavenly joy, as out of his innermost being he is privileged to enjoy the flow of those Rivers of Living Water which proceed out of the Throne of God, and whose ultimate destiny is that flowing back into God.

If, perchance, the trials of the road become heavy; we learn to find our sufficiency not in human attainment— but in that Faith, THE FAITH OF THE LORD JESUS CHRIST, which worketh by love; and which will surmount every difficulty, be it physical, material, or spiritual. This *sufficiency* can be found only in the outworking of the Indwelling Christ, for it is *in Him* and

through Him that all our needs are met.

Notes

[i] Charles S. Price, "The Story of the Conversion and Healing Ministry of Dr. Charles S. Price," *The Voice of Healing* 5:9 (December 1952): 2.

[ii] Charles S. Price, *The Story of My Life* (Pasadena, CA: Charles S. Price Publishing Co., 1935), 5.

[iii] 1917 U.S. draft registration card reveals all prior military service.

[iv] I was not able to confirm the years or degree attainment from either Wesley College or Oxford due to record losses during WWII.

[v] Price, *The Story of My Life*, 7.

[vi] Allan Line's *S.S. Ionian* passenger list, September 1906.

[vii] *List or Manifest of Alien Passengers Applying for Admission to the U.S. from a Foreign Contiguous Territory,* Washington State Ports, March 1907.

[viii] Price, *The Story of My Life*, 14.

[ix] Ibid., 15.

[x] Tim Enloe, personal interview with Bessie Price's niece, Evelyn Christian, June 9, 1999.

[xi] Price, *The Story of My Life*, 19.

[xii] Charles S. Price, "How I Received the Baptism of the Holy Spirit," *Golden Grain* 4:8 (October 1929): 7.

[xiii] Ibid.

[xiv] From an undated newspaper clipping in Price's early personal scrapbook.

[xv] Charles S. Price, U.S. military registration card, 1916.

[xvi] From an undated newspaper clipping in Price's early personal scrapbook.

[xvii] Ibid.

[xviii] Ibid.

[xix] "Church Listings," *Oakland Tribune* (Oakland, CA), Oct. 20, 1917.

[xx] Willard Peirce, audio of Rev. Peirce's recollections of Charles S. Price, no date.

[xxi] Charles S. Price, "The Ark is Coming Up the Road," *Golden Grain* 2:6 (August 1927): 8.

[xxii] Charles S. Price, "How I Received the Baptism of the Holy Spirit," *Golden Grain* 4:8 (October 1929): 8.

[xxiii] Ibid.

[xxiv] In his earliest account of this ("Our Personal Testimony" [tract] *Words of Life No. 642* (Framingham, MA: Christian Workers Union, October 7, 1922), Price recalls that he did not give an altar call for 14 years.

[xxv] "Pastor Quits Pulpit for Lecture Platform," *Oakland Tribune* (Oakland, CA), March 14, 1920.

[xxvi] Charles S. Price, "Our Personal Testimony" [tract] *Words of Life No. 642* (Framingham, MA: Christian Workers Union, October 7, 1922), 2.

[xxvii] Peirce audio.

[xxviii] William Keeney Towner, "An After That Experience," *Golden Grain* 1:7 (September 1926): 22.

[xxix] Charles S. Price, "Our Personal Testimony," 3.

[xxx] Ibid.

[xxxi] Price, *The Story of My Life*, 25.

[xxxii] Ibid., 26.

[xxxiii] Ibid., 27.

[xxxiv] Price, "Our Personal Testimony," 5.

[xxxv] Ibid.

[xxxvi] Ibid.

[xxxvii] Ibid., 6.

[xxxviii] Ibid.

[xxxix] Ibid.

[xl] Peirce audio.

[xli] Ibid.

[xlii] Price, *The Story of My Life*, 32.

[xliii] Price, "How I Received the Baptism of the Holy Spirit," 8-9.

[xliv] Ibid., 8.

[xlv] Ibid., 10.

[xlvi] Ibid.

[xlvii] Ibid., 11.

[xlviii] Ibid.

[xlix] Ibid., 13.

[l] Price, *The Story of My Life*, 38.

[li] Charles S. Price, "Testimony of Dr. C. S. Price," *Bridal Call* 6:5 (October 1922): 12.

[lii] Price, *The Story of My Life*, 52.

[liii] Price, "Testimony of Dr. C. S. Price," 13.

[liv] Ibid.

[lv] Charles S. Price, "My Call," *Golden Grain* 15:3 (June 1940): 6.

[lvi] Tim Enloe, personal interview with Dr. Edward Miller, son of B. C. Miller, August 17, 1999. Dr. Edward Miller had vivid memories of the Ashland campaign and of Price's long-term friendship with the Miller family. Miller is a missionary to Argentina and was instrumental in the great Tommy Hicks campaign there in the 1950s.

[lvii] "Revival Campaign to Begin Sunday," *Ashland Daily Tidings* (Ashland, OR), Sept. 1, 1922, 1.

[lviii] "Evangelist to be in Ashland Another Week," *Ashland Daily Tidings* (Ashland, OR), Sept. 22, 1922, 1.

[lix] "Divine Healings Attract 3000 to Chautauqua Bldg.," *Ashland Daily Tidings* (Ashland, OR), Sept. 9, 1922.

[lx] "Evangelist to be in Ashland Another Week," *Ashland Daily Tidings*, (Ashland, OR), Sept. 22, 1922, 1.

[lxi] "Medford Day is Huge Success for Dr. Price," *Ashland Daily Tidings*, (Ashland, OR), Sept. 29, 1922, 1.

[lxii] D. Mark Buntain, *Why He is a Pentecostal Preacher* (Toronto, ON: Full Gospel Publishing House, 1944), 86-90.

[lxiii] Price, *The Story of My Life, 50.*

[lxiv] Lorne F. Fox, "The Charles S. Price Story," *World Pentecost* (Issue 3, 1973): 24.

[lxv] "300 Prostrate at Once," *The Evening Telegram* (Toronto, ON), October 4, 1924.

[lxvi] "8,000 Present," *Free Press Evening Bulletin* (Winnipeg, MB), August 13, 1924.

[lxvii] "Lame Arise," *Free Press Evening Bulletin* (Winnipeg, MB), August 16, 1924.

[lxviii] "Cripple Walks," *Vancouver Daily World* (Vancouver, BC), May 16, 1923, 1.

[lxix] "Deaf and Dumb Converse," *East St. Louis Daily Journal* (East St. Louis, IL), February 18, 1925, 1.

[lxx] "Prayer Restores Sight," *The World Pointer* (Oklahoma City, OK), Aug. 23, 1931, 1.

[lxxi] Price, *The Story of My Life,* 54.

[lxxii] Nickel, Thomas, *The Shakarian Story* (Costa Mesa, CA: FGBMFI, 1964), 18.

[lxxiii] Audio interview of Kathryn Kuhlman and Myrtle Parrott by Jamie Buckingham, Billy Graham Center Archives, Wheaton College, Wheaton, IL, December 1974.

[lxxiv] John W. Carver, personal interview of T. L. Osborn, May 11, 2001.

[lxxv] Charles Sydney Price, death certificate, County of Los Angeles, California, March 8, 1947.

[lxxvi] Ibid.